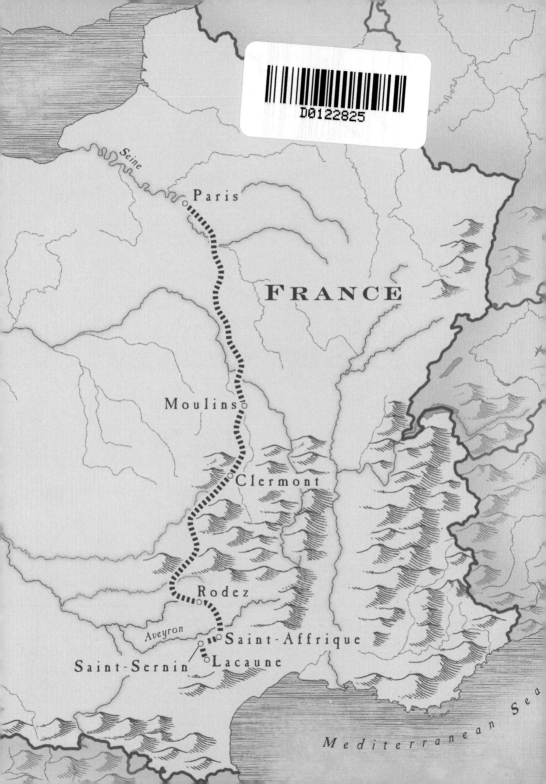

Seine

Paris

FRANCE

Moulins

Clermont

Rodez

Aveyron

Saint-Affrique

Saint-Sernin

Lacaune

Mediterranean Sea

D0122825

WILD BOY

WILD BOY

THE REAL LIFE *of* THE SAVAGE OF AVEYRON

Mary Losure

ILLUSTRATED BY *Timothy Basil Ering*

CANDLEWICK PRESS

First edition 2013

Library of Congress Catalog Card Number 2012943644
ISBN 978-0-7636-5669-0

12 13 14 15 16 17 SHD 10 9 8 7 6 5 4 3 2 1

Printed in Ann Arbor, MI, U.S.A.

This book was typeset in Centaur MT.
The illustrations were done in charcoal.

Candlewick Press
99 Dover Street
Somerville, Massachusetts 02144

visit us at www.candlewick.com

To David and Michael

M. L.

——

To you, Jen, and our two amazing wild boys

T. B. E.

· I ·

The mountains of southern France, 1797

SUMMER AND WINTER, the wild boy lived in the forest.

He dug for roots with his bare hands and searched for nuts in the dry, dead leaves on the forest floor. Poisonous mushrooms grew there, too, but the boy had learned what was safe and what wasn't. Before he ate anything, he sniffed it.

He went naked, like an animal. But he walked upright, like a human.

Animal trails led like green tunnels through the underbrush, but if the boy followed them, he always kept in mind where a stream was, for when he was thirsty, he had to find water. He had no way to carry it: no water jar or animal skin.

He had no tools. No fire.

He was (as nearly as anyone could figure out later) about nine years old.

Under his chin he bore a long, straight scar, slashed across his throat as though someone had tried to kill him and left him for dead in the forest. Yet somehow, the wild boy had survived.

In wintertime his bare feet left tracks in the snow, but no one seemed to notice them. If he came upon a tiny clearing and a peasant's stone cottage, he didn't show himself. If he smelled the smoke from woodcutters' fires, he stayed hidden. Season after season passed, and no one knew about the boy living all by himself in the woods.

In places the forest gave way to rocky heights where blueberries ripened in the sun. If the wild boy scrambled up the rocks, he could see the distant ridges that circled all around him, as though he were standing in a bowl. What lay beyond, he had no way of knowing.

Below the lookout rocks, in a river valley just visible through the treetops, lay a village called Lacaune.

Sounds carried far in that valley: a rooster crowing, a dog barking, or a cowbell clanging. But if the wild boy heard them, he stayed far away. He loped through the trees and was gone.

· I I ·

Everyone came . . . to see the child that was said to be a wild beast.

— J.-J. Constans-Saint-Estève, January 1800

ONE DAY IN THE VILLAGE OF LACAUNE, a couple of peasants returned from the woods with a strange story. They'd seen a naked boy crouched on the forest floor, his hands digging through the leaves for something to eat. They'd watched, curious. But they hadn't caught him.

So the wild boy's life in the woods went on.

In the mornings, he could watch as mist gathered in the mountain valleys before it faded in the sunlight. He could listen to rain pattering on the tree leaves. He could wake from sleep to see the round moon filling the night woods with light and shadows. A whole year passed as it always did in the forest.

Until one day, when the wild boy was about ten . . .

A group of woodsmen spotted him, and somehow, they caught him. He fought and bit, but it did no good. They took him to Lacaune and led him to the town square. It was paved with river rocks, bumpy beneath the wild boy's bare feet. At its center, an ancient fountain splashed. All around, the tall houses of village merchants made a wall that blocked out the mountains.

Villagers gathered around the wild boy, jabbering in words he didn't understand. Women washing their laundry in the stone troughs nearby set it aside and hurried over to see.

No one alive today knows the details of what happened next — whether the woodsmen kept a rope around the wild boy's neck or tied his hands behind his back. No one knows

if that night, they took him somewhere to sleep or left him in the square, tied and helpless. But every day, he was forced to stand, hour after hour, for everyone to see.

And maybe it was then that the wild boy began to hate the staring eyes of crowds.

But at last (exactly how, no one knows) he got loose. He ran for the forest and was free again.

His time as a prisoner had taught him something, though: where there were people, there was food.

Now sometimes when he was hungry, he visited the farm fields on the edge of the village. With the safety of the forest behind him, he dug for potatoes and turnips. Sometimes he carried them back into the woods. Other times he ate them where he stood.

When autumn came, the ferns on the forest floor withered to brown. The trees turned red and gold. Soon frost would touch the fields with white and the first snowflakes would swirl from the sky, but the wild boy could live through winter in the forest.

He'd done it for a long time.

The snow melted, and in the pale sunlight, wildflowers bloomed on the forest floor. The oaks and beeches put on their new leaves. Summer came, and the forest was shady again, dense and deep.

On July 25, 1799, when the wild boy was around eleven years old, he was captured again.

This time, it was three hunters who spotted him, and perhaps they had dogs, for the wild boy climbed a tree. The hunters caught him anyway, tied him up tight, and marched him down the mountain to Lacaune.

And this time, he wasn't put on display. Instead, the hunters took him to stay with a poor old widow who lived in a little cottage just behind the Lacaune village square.

Why they chose her, no one knows. Perhaps she was the only one in the village who would take in a strange, wild boy.

Stories told later said she made him wear a shirt to cover his nakedness, but if she did, it couldn't have been easy, for the wild boy *hated* clothes. Perhaps she was a gentle, patient person who was kind to him and he wore a shirt to please her. Or maybe the hunters forced the scratching, biting boy into a shirt he couldn't get off. The peasants' stories offer no clues.

They do say the widow seemed to like the wild boy.

She offered him meat, both raw and cooked in an iron pot over the fire, but he wouldn't eat it. When she gave him acorns, he sniffed them first, then ate them. After sniffing them, he ate chestnuts, walnuts, and potatoes, too.

The walls of the widow's cottage, like the other cottages in Lacaune, were made of stone. Dim light came through the tiny windows.

Maybe once—so long ago that he had forgotten all but

the faintest memory — the wild boy had lived in a cottage much like this one.

Maybe, as the widow tended her cooking fire or swept her hearth with her hazel-twig broom, the wild boy watched her, trying to remember his own mother, his own home.

Eight days passed.

But the wild boy's real home, now, wasn't a cottage. It was the woods, the wind, the night stars, and the moon shining down.

So the wild boy escaped again.

This time he climbed the mountain slopes until the village was far below him, its gray stone roofs growing smaller the higher he climbed. When he reached the summit, he loped down the other side into another valley. Ahead of him lay more mountains.

Now, in this new country, the wild boy seemed to have less fear of strangers.

Sometimes when he saw a peasant's cottage, he would walk right up to it and go inside.

There he would stand, a thin, wild-haired boy dressed only in a tattered and dirty shirt. Perhaps the peasants were curious, or maybe they pitied him, but in any case they gave him food.

And when they offered him potatoes, he did something no one seems to have noticed him doing before: he would put them into the fire to cook. Maybe he had learned that from watching the old lady, but in any case, he wasn't very patient. He'd pull them from the fire, eat them when they were still burning hot, and be out the door.

As the summer days passed, he roamed the countryside, visiting isolated farms and stopping several times at one farm where the people were particularly nice to him.

In time, he worked his way down the mountain slopes. Ahead of him lay a long, low saddle of land. The wild boy loped across it, through stony fields where peasants grew rye for their coarse, black bread. Along the walls and hedges that divided one field from another grew blackberries and wild plums. Perhaps he stopped to sniff them first, before he ate them.

Now all around him lay a landscape of fields and woods. On distant hills, the spires of village churches poked the sky. Beyond lay more hills: the world unfolding into the blue distance.

The wild boy could see far now that he'd left the forest — but he could also be seen. Soon, peasants in the area began talking about a strange new visitor.

Later, a man from the French government, a commissioner named Guiraud, rode his horse deep into that same country and asked people there about the wild boy.

They told him stories of how the boy swam in streams and climbed trees, dug in the fields for food, and could run very fast on all fours.

And people said, too, that when the mountain winds

blew, the wild boy looked at the sky, made sounds deep in his throat, and gave great bursts of laughter.

The days grew shorter. When fall ended, bitter cold set in, the coldest winter in many years.

On January 8, 1800, the wild boy was coming down a narrow, steep-sided valley when it took a sharp turn. There, in front of him through the bare trees, loomed a tall white building with a red tile roof and wooden balconies. Around it, carved into the steep sides of the valley, lay vegetable gardens. Could there be potatoes or turnips beneath the cold earth?

He loped forward, crouched down, and began to dig.

He was caught (it's said by the back of his tattered shirt) by the man who owned the building, a tanner named Vidal.

But what did it matter, really? He'd always escaped before. Surely he could do it again.

*I will shortly send you an official report containing in detail
the circumstances under which the child was brought into my
hands, the information I have acquired concerning his existence,
and the grounds for considering him an extraordinary being.*

— J.-J. Constans-Saint-Estève, January 1800

THE TANNER TOOK HIM INSIDE the building, which
lay on the outskirts of a village named Saint-Sernin. Before
long, everyone in the village ran to see. Among them was a village official named J.-J. Constans-Saint-Estève.

"I found him seated in front of a fire that appeared to give
him great pleasure," the man wrote. But he noticed that from

time to time, the boy seemed uneasy with so many people around.

Constans-Saint-Estève came closer. He began to ask the wild boy questions, but got no reply. The village official spoke louder, but still the wild boy was silent.

The strange boy's eyes shone with intelligence, Constans-Saint-Estève remembered years later. But there was something in his expression that the man couldn't quite read.

Constans-Saint-Estève felt sorry for the wild boy, but he was also curious about him. More curious, it seemed, than anyone else who had seen him so far. The man was also, as a village official, the kind of person who was used to getting his way.

So Constans-Saint-Estève decided to take the wild boy home with him.

He took the boy's hand, kindly, and tried to lead him toward the door, but the wild boy "resisted vigorously," Constans-Saint-Estève wrote later.

Yet when Constans-Saint-Estève patted him and kissed him and smiled at him in a friendly way, the wild boy suddenly seemed to change his mind. He let the man lead him out the door. Trailed by curious villagers, the two of them walked down the narrow valley.

Soon they came to a river. A mill wheel turned in the water, creaking in the cold air. Above them, the village of Saint-Sernin perched high on the cliffs on the other side of the river.

Constans-Saint-Estève and the wild boy crossed a stone bridge, then climbed steep steps cut into the rock. When they reached the village, they walked through a maze of streets until they came to a tall, narrow house crowded among all the others atop the cliffs. The man opened the door, and the wild boy went inside.

A servant brought an earthenware plate of food piled with meat, both cooked and raw, along with rye bread and wheat bread, apples, pears, grapes, walnuts, chestnuts, acorns, parsnips, an orange, and some potatoes.

The wild boy picked up each kind of food, sniffed at it, and refused to eat anything but the potatoes. These he threw into the fire, then snatched them out again and ate them hot.

Constans-Saint-Estève told the servant to get more potatoes, and the wild boy seemed happy to see them.

When he was done eating, the wild boy looked around the room. He took Constans-Saint-Estève's hand, led him to a pitcher of water, and rapped on it. When the servant brought wine instead of water, the boy wouldn't drink it. He showed "great impatience," Constans-Saint-Estève later recalled, until he was given water.

Then, having eaten and drunk his fill, the wild boy bolted out the door.

He ran swiftly, but the town of Saint-Sernin, high on its rock, was no easy place to escape from. The houses formed impassible walls, and they were hung with balconies from which anyone could spot a boy on the run. Many streets came to dead ends or led to cliffs, high above the river. Constans-Saint-Estève chased behind, yelling.

"I had a hard time catching him," Constans-Saint-Estève wrote later, but once captured, the wild boy let himself be led back to the house. The whole way back, he kept his face still, showing no signs of either pleasure or displeasure. Curious, the man began watching the wild boy more and more carefully.

What was the wild boy thinking?

He was content with simple things, Constans-Saint-Estève noticed. He would hold an acorn in his hand for the longest time, gazing at it as though the mere sight of it made him happy. Constans-Saint-Estève wrote that the boy had an "air of satisfaction that nothing could trouble."

Nothing, that is, except being trapped inside the house.

The wild boy tried to find ways to escape, but Constans-Saint-Estève was always watching him. The wild boy had no way of knowing the reason, but it was this: Constans-Saint-Estève wanted to see if this odd boy really *was* what the peasants claimed: a truly wild human being.

Why did that matter?

It mattered because Constans-Saint-Estève, who had once lived in the great and faraway city of Paris, knew that scientists there would be very, very interested in studying a real wild human.

So Constans-Saint-Estève observed the wild boy closely all that day, and the next.

Then he got out his official government stationery, dipped a quill pen in an inkpot, and began a letter. It was addressed to the administrators of the nearest orphanage, which was in a small town called Saint-Affrique.

"I have ordered brought to your orphanage . . . an unidentified child," he wrote. "In every respect, this interesting and unfortunate being invites the care of humanity, perhaps even the attention of a philanthropic observer." ("Philanthropic

observer" was another way of saying scientist.) "I am informing the government," he added, noting that the government
would most likely decide to have the wild boy sent to Paris.

"Would you see to it that all possible care is provided,"
the letter went on. "Have the child watched during the day
and bedded for the night in a room from which he cannot
escape."

When the *gendarmes* (military policemen) came to the door of
Constans-Saint-Estève's house, they wore stiff blue-and-red
coats, tall black boots, and long swords. They took the wild
boy away with them, and they cannot have been very gentle
about it, because afterward, he hated men in uniforms.

All day, he was jostled and jolted as the horses made their
way down the slopes of Saint-Sernin, then galloped down the
road toward Saint-Affrique. The town lay at the end of a wide
valley, beyond which lay more mountains.

As night fell, the *gendarmes* reined in their horses on swampy ground by a wide river. Through a set of stone gateposts, they entered a walled garden. At its far end sat the dark hulk of a building — the orphanage of Saint-Affrique.

The next day — January 11, 1800 — a new entry was added to the list of names in the orphanage's admittance book.

A young savage, found in the woods near Saint-Sernin. Deaf and mute.

The wild boy was *not* deaf, as people at the orphanage soon discovered. But they must have wondered: If he wasn't really deaf, maybe he wasn't really wild, either? For this is what they did next: They took the wild boy outside and led him to an open field, bare in the wintertime. Beyond it, the mountains loomed.

And then they let him loose.

"He took to running on all fours," a man at the orphanage wrote later. "If we had not followed him closely and overtaken him, he would soon have reached the mountain and disappeared."

Instead, he was led back to the grim, gray building.

Within the orphanage's stone walls, there were sometimes tiny babies abandoned by their parents. Sometimes brothers and sisters appeared on its doorstep, stayed until they were ten or twelve, then went out into the world to seek their fortunes. Their names were written in a big, thick roll book, the dates recorded under columns labeled "Entered" and "Left." For those who weren't lucky enough to leave, there was a third column: "Dead."

But at that particular time, the winter of 1800, the wild boy seems to have been the only child there. The roll book then shows only grown-ups: people living in a building that served not only as an orphanage, but also as a hospital and a poorhouse. They included wounded soldiers, villagers who were sick or old, a woman who was "feeble in spirit," and a nameless, homeless man picked up in the town square.

Now all of them could gaze with surprise at the newest arrival—a wild boy.

"His eyes are dark and full of life," an orphanage administrator wrote. "He searches incessantly for a means of escape."

They offered him bread, but he smelled it, bit it, and threw it away. "We made him a gown of gray linen," the orphanage administrator wrote. "He does not know how to get it off, but this garment annoys him greatly. We have just let him free in the garden. Wanting to escape, he tried to break one of the strips of wood in the gate. He never speaks. When he is given potatoes, he takes as many as his pretty little hands can hold. If the potatoes are cooked (he prefers them thus), he peels them and eats them like a monkey. He has a pleasing laugh. If you take his potatoes away from him, he lets out sharp cries."

The man wrote that the wild boy appeared to be about twelve years old, at most.

· IV ·

From external appearance, this child is no different from any other.
He is 136 centimeters [four feet six inches] tall. . . . He has a
light complexion . . . a round face; he has dark deep-set eyes; long
eyelashes; brown hair; a long, somewhat pointed nose; an average
mouth; a round chin; an agreeable [expression]; and a pleasant smile.

— Pierre-Joseph Bonnaterre, *Historical Notice on the Savage of Aveyron*, 1800

IN THE GREAT CATHEDRAL TOWN OF RODEZ, just

a few days' journey north of the orphanage, lived a thin-faced,

long-nosed professor named Pierre-Joseph Bonnaterre. He

was a priest but also a scientist, which in those times was not

unusual. And one day, the news reached him that a wild boy

had been discovered in the woods and was now not far from Rodez.

Bonnaterre, who taught natural history at a school for boys, was very, very interested.

Like other naturalists, Bonnaterre examined plants and animals, compared them with others, and fit them into categories. Birds were creatures to be captured and preserved, stuffed, with tufts of cotton where their eyes had been and labels hung from their tiny claws. Butterflies were specimens to be taken by their bright wings and stuck through with pins. A portrait of Bonnaterre shows him sitting very upright at his desk, wearing a tight collar and a cold, slightly pained expression. A collection of specimens lies at his elbow: a shell, a snake, and a small, wide-eyed fish that, if not yet dead, soon would be.

Now the professor hoped to have something new to study.

Why should scientists in *Paris* get the first chance? Bonnaterre was closer, and quicker. He went to see a government official and asked to have the wild boy sent to Rodez's Central School, where Bonnaterre was a teacher.

And so it was that the next part of the wild boy's life began.

The wild boy had been in the orphanage for three weeks when, on a February morning of the year 1800, a carriage and driver pulled up to the stone gates. When it drove away again, the boy was inside.

All that day and the next, the carriage jolted through winter-bare fields and forests until at last it came to a great hill. At its crest stood two pale, square towers, tall against the sky: the great cathedral of Rodez.

The carriage labored up the hill, past the fortress-like stone walls that surrounded the city. Soon, it rolled into the public square at the foot of the cathedral. From the cathedral's heights, gargoyles grinned down.

The carriage clattered along twisted, narrow streets till it stopped at the carved stone entranceway of the Rodez Central School.

As the wild boy stepped down from the carriage, gawkers swarmed all around.

Eyes stared at him as they had, long ago now, in the village square in Lacaune. Faces jabbered. Bodies crowded in tight, shoving and jostling. . . .

And when they came too close, the wild boy bit them.

"It was only with some difficulty that he was led within the confines of the Central School," an official wrote. The school's huge wooden doors creaked open. Strangers hurried the wild boy through.

Then the doors swung shut behind him.

What is it like to be treated not as a person, but as a specimen?

The wild boy would soon find out.

Professor Bonnaterre examined the wild boy's body, taking careful measurements.

"When he raises his head, there will be seen . . . a horizontal scar of some 41 millimeters in length, which seems to be the scar of a wound made with a cutting instrument," Bonnaterre wrote. (This line ——————————— is 41 millimeters long.)

The professor counted the burns on the wild boy's face. "There is one on the right eyebrow; another in the middle of the cheek on the same side; another on the chin; and another on the left cheek," he wrote. Bonnaterre noted down the six long slashes that ran the whole length of the boy's arm. "His whole body is covered with scars," Bonnaterre wrote.

He didn't bother to write down the expression on the boy's face as he was poked and prodded and measured.

The professor did wonder whether the scar on the wild boy's throat was evidence that someone had tried to kill him and left him for dead in the forest. "Did some barbaric hand, having led the child into the wilds, strike him with a death-dealing blade?" he asked. But nowhere, in all the long report he was later to write, would he show a glimmer of sympathy

or a shred of affection for the motherless, fatherless boy who was now in his care.

Bonnaterre gave the boy a label—the Savage of Aveyron—and made careful observations on how the Savage's habits and manner compared with those of other wild children found in historical records: a boy found living with wolves in Germany in 1544; a boy discovered among bears in Lithuania in 1661; a boy in Ireland who lived with a flock of sheep, year not given; and five wild boys and three wild girls found in various places in Europe throughout the 1700s.

Some scientists actually believed that such wild children belonged to a different species, *Homo ferus,* or Wild Man.

If they *did* belong to a whole different species, and the wild boy was one of them . . . was he even a human being?

Bonnaterre stared at him, trying to decide.

The professor made the wild boy take a series of tests.

In one, Bonnaterre held a mirror in front of the boy's face.

At first, to try to find the person he saw in the mirror, the wild boy looked behind it. When that didn't work, he brought his gaze back to the mirror. Beside his own reflection, the boy saw someone holding a potato. The wild boy reached toward the mirror, but he couldn't get the potato that way. Then, without turning his head, he reached behind him and grabbed it.

It was clever of the wild boy to get the potato by recognizing, almost instantly, how a mirror works.

Still, Bonnaterre decided that didn't matter much.

In another test, he had music played — violins, perhaps, viola and cello and maybe a flute or two — and watched what happened next.

"The sounds of the most harmonious instruments . . . make no impression on his ear, or at least he appears to be insensitive to them," Bonnaterre wrote, "and he shows no perception of the noises made next to him; but if a cupboard that contains his favorite foods is opened, if walnuts, to which he is very partial, are cracked behind him . . . he will turn around to seize them."

Not being interested in music, but paying attention to the creak of a cupboard door or the crack of a walnut—Bonnaterre considered that a black mark against the wild boy.

And there was worse to come.

"He has been seen, when tired, to walk on all fours," Bonnaterre wrote.

It was, to Bonnaterre, a very important point. God and Man ("Man" was what scientists in those days called all human beings) walked upright, of course.

Only dumb beasts walked on all fours.

When he wasn't being poked and prodded and tested, the wild boy could wander where he wanted inside the Central School.

It was an ancient stone building built around a

courtyard and walled garden. Above each classroom entrance, the name of a subject was carved in stone. "Rhetoric," said one. "Humanities," said the writing above another doorway, but no one expected the wild boy to walk through it. A classroom, after all, was no place for a child like a wild beast.

What the school's students thought of the wild boy or how he acted when he saw them was something no one will ever know, for it was never written down. Alone, in his bare feet and a rough tunic and leather belt that he was not allowed to take off, the wild boy padded down the long, cold corridors.

Spiral staircases led up to the school's second and third stories. Some of the windows overlooked the central garden. Others had a view of the city streets. At one end of the school stood a round tower. If he climbed it, the boy could gaze out over the rooftops to open fields and woodlands.

Then one day, someone left the door to the outside world open . . . and the wild boy was out and running.

The streets were like dark stone tunnels with only a crack of light from above. But if the wild boy could reach the fields and woods, the sky would open wide! The gray city and the Central School would be left behind forever!

But in his odd costume and bare feet in the dead of winter, he was instantly recognizable as the Savage of Aveyron. He was spotted, caught, and brought back.

"He is always looking to escape and takes advantage of every occasion on which he finds the door open to get away," Bonnaterre wrote. "He has already escaped four or five times from Rodez; but happily he was always retaken, sometimes at considerable distance from the town."

The wild boy broke every window in his room, but they replaced them with linen too tough to tear. Once, he jumped from a second-story window. But whatever he did, it was no use; he was always caught.

He was angry sometimes, Bonnaterre noted coldly. If someone made him mad, he'd make cries of rage or even give the person a sudden, well-aimed bite. Sometimes he'd place his closed fists over his eyes and hit himself, hard, in the head.

He took to spending hours alone in his room. "When it is time to go to bed, nothing can stop him," Bonnaterre wrote. "He takes a torch; he points to the key to his room, and he becomes furious if not obeyed."

"His sleep is very light," Bonnaterre noted, "and he wakes at the slightest knock on the door. When the wind of the Midi [the mountain wind] blows, his bursts of laughter can be heard during the night and, from time to time, other vocal sounds that express neither pain nor pleasure."

Most mornings, the wild boy woke at dawn. He would wrap himself in his blanket, head and all, and begin rocking. Back and forth he rocked, hour after hour.

Sometimes his face contorted as though he were having a seizure. Deep in his throat, the boy made a humming sound, a kind of dull murmur.

· **V** ·

This eagerness to warm up and the pleasure he displays near a fire
made me suspect that the child had never lived, as some would
have it, in a state of absolute nakedness during a winter as severe
as the one that we have just experienced.

—Pierre-Joseph Bonnaterre, *Historical Notice on the Savage of Aveyron,* 1800

SNOW DRIFTED DOWN, past the leering gargoyles and
frosted windows of the city. Inside the Central School, the
only warm place was by the fire.

The wild boy was drawn to fires. They made him roar with
laughter and shake his hands in signs of joy. The boy would
lift his tunic as high as his leather belt so he could feel the

warmth on his bare skin. If someone yelled, "For shame!" he'd drop it, Bonnaterre wrote. But a minute later, he'd lift it again.

Bonnaterre had heard the stories of how the wild boy had wandered naked and barefoot through the woods in the dead of winter, but now, watching the boy toast his bare bottom at the fire, he began to doubt them. "I could not imagine how an individual who had tolerated such severe cold could also be so sensitive to impressions of heat," he wrote. Could it really be true that the wild boy didn't feel the cold?

So Bonnaterre devised an experiment to find out.

"One evening, with the thermometer at four degrees below zero [25 degrees Fahrenheit] I undressed him completely and he appeared glad indeed to be rid of these garments," Bonnaterre wrote. "Next I pretended to take him out into the open air; I took him by the hand through the long corridors, up to the main door of the school building."

It was the same door through which the wild boy had tried to escape so many times before.

Now the sour, unsmiling man who was always staring at him had, for some reason, freed him from his hated tunic and the leather belt that held it tight. Now the man who never let him go was *leading him outside!*

"Instead of showing any reluctance to follow me, he dragged me out of doors by repeated yanks," Bonnaterre wrote.

The dark, empty streets lay before them, and beyond that, the open fields. *The forest!*

Freedom.

And yet . . . the man would not let him free.

Another night, Bonnaterre crept silently into the wild boy's room. The boy was asleep on his bed of straw, wrapped only in a linen sheet.

He lay curled up in a ball, with his fists jammed into his eyes and his face against his knees.

It must have been a sad sight, the wild boy curled up so

tight against the world, but the scientist didn't seem to feel any sympathy.

Instead, he ran his hands over the boy's arms and legs to see if they were cold to the touch.

They weren't, though. They were "comfortably warm."

So it was true!

Two separate experiments had proved it to Bonnaterre's satisfaction: the wild boy *didn't* feel the cold. "He can be indifferent to the impressions of cold and [still] find pleasure in the gentle effects of heat, since we see dogs and cats with the same habits," Bonnaterre wrote.

But what was it like for the wild boy, Bonnaterre's latest experiment?

The boy's burns and cuts and the slash across his neck had come from somewhere, even if he tried hard to forget them. And surely, the pain he'd suffered had left traces deep inside him.

Maybe, sometimes, he dreamed about a burning stick, jabbing at him. A knife blade, flashing.

And that night, when he felt Bonnaterre's hand creeping over his body, did the boy wake to see a black shape looming over him in the dark?

Was he filled with terror?

Did it give him nightmares later?

It was no concern of Bonnaterre's. After all, to him, the boy was only a specimen.

But there was one person who didn't test the wild boy, or stare at him, or do experiments on him.

His name was Clair Saussol. He was the gardener at the Central School, but he'd also been chosen to be the wild boy's caretaker. He was sixty-four years old and had come to Rodez from a tiny village in the countryside.

Clair Saussol was what educated people often referred to as a "simple peasant." It's likely he couldn't read or write

more than his own name. Because he was "only" a peasant, not much was ever written down about him.

But after a while, the boy began to follow Clair around like a puppy.

When spring came, Clair had soil to dig and seeds to plant, so most likely the wild boy would have gone with him to the garden. The boy's lively dark eyes would have watched Clair as he turned the earth, releasing its rich spring scent. The boy would have watched as Clair's workingman's hands, as lined with dirt as his own, dropped in the seeds.

Beans, perhaps, or the flat, pale seeds of cucumbers.

The wild boy sometimes buried food to dig up later. Now, here in the garden, Clair was doing something very similar!

When the old man took up his spade and shuffled to another part of the garden, maybe the wild boy trotted after him to see what he'd do next.

◆ ◆ ◆

Meeting Clair was one good thing at the Central School. Another was discovering different kinds of food.

"He was constantly occupied during his stay at Rodez in shelling green beans; and he fulfilled this task with an expertise appropriate to the most practiced man," Bonnaterre noticed.

On his left, the wild boy piled the dried bean plants, with their pods, and on his right he put a pot to cook them in. "He opened the pods one after the other with an inimitable suppleness of movement," Bonnaterre wrote. "As he emptied the pods, he piled them up next to him symmetrically: and when his work was through, he took away the pot, added water, and put it next to the fire which he fueled with the pods he had piled up. If the fire was out, he took the shovel and placed it in the hands of Clair, signaling him to go looking for some nearby coals."

The wild boy discovered that potatoes didn't always have to be roasted in a fire: he also liked them cooked in other ways. "When he felt like eating hash-browned potatoes, he chose the largest, brought them to the first person he found in the kitchen, tendered a knife to cut them into slices, went to find a frying pan, and pointed out the cupboard where the cooking oil was stored."

After a while, when the wild boy went to the kitchen, he lifted every pot lid to see what was underneath it.

Instead of sniffing meat and rejecting it the way he had before, he tasted some — and discovered that he liked both meat and meat broth. When he found a pot of broth, he waited until the cook's back was turned to dip in a piece of bread. Then he'd pop it in his mouth. "I saw him do [it] one day five or six times in a row without being caught," Bonnaterre wrote.

One day the wild boy got a taste of sausage, and instantly it became one of his favorite foods.

The next day, wrote Bonnaterre, "a captain of the auxiliary battalion of Aveyron, who was dining in the room where the child was, signaled him to approach, by showing him a little piece of sausage he had cut from a larger piece on his plate; the young man approached to accept the offer. . . . With his left hand he took the morsel that the captain held between his fingers; with the other hand, he adroitly seized the rest of the sausage on the plate."

As the boy scampered away with his prize, maybe the captain thought it was funny, but Bonnaterre didn't seem to.

He recorded the incident solemnly, one more observation along with all the others he was collecting about this strange creature, this possible *Homo ferus.*

Bonnaterre had noticed that the wild boy followed Clair from place to place, but he didn't think that meant the boy actually *liked* Clair. "His affections are as limited as his knowledge," Bonnaterre decided. "If he shows some preference for his caretaker," he wrote, "it is an expression of need and not the sentiment of gratitude; he follows the man because the latter is concerned with satisfying his needs."

Bonnaterre didn't think the wild boy was very bright, either. In fact, Bonnaterre suspected he was the kind of person that scientists in those days called an "imbecile."

"Suspicion of imbecility," Bonnaterre wrote in his report, and he tallied up what he'd observed, the results of the many tests the wild boy never knew he was taking.

"This child is not totally without intelligence . . . ; however, we are obliged to say that . . . we find only purely animal function: if he has sensations, they do not give rise to ideas. . . . He reflects on nothing."

The boy had "no imagination, no memory," the professor wrote. "This state of imbecility is reflected in his gaze, for he does not fix his attention on any object; . . . in his gait, for he always walks at a trot or a gallop; in his actions, for they lack purpose and determination."

Whether it was true or false, fair or unfair, Bonnaterre's verdict would soon be written down for all the world to see: the wild boy was, mostly likely, an imbecile.

By mid-July, the gardens in the courtyard of the Central School basked in the warm sun. Beans hung on the vines for the picking, but the wild boy would not be there to shell them. For an official order had come from Paris.

A group of Paris scientists calling themselves the Society of Observers of Man wanted *their* chance to study the wild boy. One of them had gone to see the French Minister of the Interior, a man named Lucien Bonaparte. Lucien Bonaparte was the brother of the mighty Napoléon Bonaparte, the ruler (soon to be emperor) of France.

The Minister had written a letter demanding to have the "unfortunate boy" sent to Paris. "I claim him," Lucien Bonaparte had written to officials at Rodez, "and request that you send him to me forthwith."

The Minister had sent the letter months ago, back in the

winter, but by the time it reached Rodez, the wild boy was already at the Central School. The Minister had decided to let him stay there for a time, but now that time was up.

That July, in the year 1800, the Minister sent another order, commanding Professor Bonnaterre to bring the wild boy to a special school in Paris. The Institute for Deaf-Mutes, as it was then called, was for children who couldn't hear or speak, who were known in those days as "deaf-mutes."

It was run by one of the members of the Society of Observers of Man, a man named Abbé (*abbé* is a French word for priest) Roche-Ambroise Cucurron Sicard.

Who was, it seemed, quite eager to meet the wild boy of Aveyron.

·VI·

*Provided that the state of imbecility we have noticed in this child
places no obstacle in the way of his instruction . . . every success
may be hoped for from that philosopher-teacher [Abbé Sicard,
of the Paris Institute for Deaf-Mutes] who has worked such
miracles in this kind of education.*

—Pierre-Joseph Bonnaterre, *Historical Notice on the Savage of Aveyron*, 1800

AS HE SAT IN THE CARRIAGE, the wild boy wore
the same rough tunic and leather belt he always did. His feet,
as usual, were bare. Beside him on the carriage seat was a little
sack packed with a few familiar foods: rye bread, potatoes,
beans, and walnuts.

It was July 20, 1800, and the wild boy, Bonnaterre, and

Clair were on their way to Paris. The wild boy didn't know that, of course. How could he, without words, understand?

The wild boy was good at reading the expressions on people's faces. But what did they mean now, the looks on Clair's kind face and Bonnaterre's cold one?

And how could the wild boy ask, using only his hands? He'd always known how to show people what he wanted—a quick rap on a pitcher for water, a finger pointed at the key to his room when he wanted to go to bed. But what is the motion for "Where are we going?" What is the gesture for "What is going to happen to me?"

Day after day, the countryside jogged by outside the carriage window.

Bonnaterre noticed that the wild boy always kept his little sack of food close to him. "Whenever we changed carriages or arrived at an inn, he stopped in front of the door and would not enter the lodgings until preceded by this object of his dearest affection," he wrote scornfully.

But how could the wild boy help wondering, *What will happen when the sack is empty?*

There are times in the wild boy's life that are hidden, as though a sudden fog swirled down, misting everything; the wild boy's long journey to Paris is one of them. If he had adventures along the way, the only one who saw them (at least, who could write things down) was a grim, narrow-nosed professor. Bonnaterre left a few clues, nothing more.

Still, from those clues, and from old maps of the time, it's possible to figure out some of what happened.

The road from Rodez led upward into more mountains, even higher and more remote than those the wild boy had come from. When he came to streams, the wild boy would lie down on his stomach and drink, "putting his chin into the water right up to his mouth," Bonnaterre noticed. Maybe it was in these wild mountains that the wild boy tried, again, to run away. "During our trip, he . . . made several unsuccessful attempts at escape," Bonnaterre noted. The professor did not say where or how the wild boy escaped, or who caught him. Was it Clair who chased after him, calling him back, pleading? Was it a villager who set after him with dogs baying in the night?

On rocky, winding roads they traveled past deep gorges and waterfalls and lonely marshes where wild birds cried. Then they descended to a plain. There, the roads were wider, paved with lava.

They came to a town called Clermont, built of the same dark stone. Its filthy streets looked like tunnels through a dunghill, a traveler there once noted; sickening smells hung so heavy in the dark, narrow lanes that the wind from the mountains could barely blow them away.

Perhaps it was in that dark, dirty city that the first gawkers began gathering. Bonnaterre wrote later that during their trip, they were pestered by "curious people who stationed themselves in crowds along our route."

But wherever it first began, the staring eyes and the jabbering faces were back.

From Clermont, the road to Paris wound through fields of golden wheat, ripe for the harvest. But as the days passed in the hot, dusty carriage, the wild boy grew listless.

As they neared the town of Moulins, about halfway to Paris, the boy began to shiver in the July heat. He wouldn't eat. When they stopped to change horses, he could hardly get up.

For the wild boy had a fearsome, dreaded disease—smallpox.

The first symptoms of smallpox are a rash, first on the face, then on the arms and legs. Then, as the disease takes hold, the rash changes to something much worse—raised, pus-filled bumps that can leave behind deep pits that scar a victim's face forever.

That is, if the person is lucky enough to survive.

Clair worried, but what could he do?

Even Bonnaterre was worried, he wrote in a letter.

Later, another scientist would write a few lines about the wild boy's sickness: "He refused to eat for two days; he was sad and troubled. He was not given any medicine."

But he was tough, that wild boy.

He'd survived many things that would have killed other people. Now smallpox was one more.

"He recovered very well in a few days," the scientist noted. When the disease had passed, the wild boy had no new scars — only his old ones, the burns and slashes he'd had for so long.

Now he barely had time to rest before being bundled back into the carriage.

In early August, eighteen days after they'd left Rodez, they neared the city of Paris. Ahead in the distance rose two sets of low hills. Between them, in a blue haze, spread a sea of slate

roofs, chimneys, and church spires. The sun had already set and the summer night was falling as the stagecoach clattered into the city.

"[He] arrived . . . at ten o'clock at night in the charge of an old serving man who has been caring for him . . . and of a professor of natural history at the Central School of Rodez, Citizen Bonnaterre," an article in one of the city's newspapers, the *Gazette de France,* announced.

"As yet we know very little about the child, who will now be the object of observations by true philosophers [a term then used to mean scientists] and who will surely be visited promptly." The scientists, the article said, would be eager to find out all they could about the wild boy, "down to the slightest movements he might make to express his first sensations, his first ideas, his first thoughts."

The newspaper noted that Professor Bonnaterre had placed the wild boy "in the hands of the Father of deaf-mutes," Abbé Sicard.

In those days, many people believed it was a miracle that so-called deaf-mutes could be taught to read or write. Abbé Sicard had become famous as a "miracle worker."

Now the Institute had a new pupil, and all of Paris was watching.

·VII·

Many people . . . believed that the education of this child would only be a question of some months, and that he would soon be able to give the most interesting information about his past life.

—Jean-Marc-Gaspard Itard, *The Wild Boy of Aveyron*

WHEN THE WILD BOY ARRIVED at the Institute for Deaf-Mutes, he lay down on the ground and went to sleep. Abbé Sicard woke him up and offered him bread, but the wild boy wouldn't eat. Instead, he made motions to the Abbé that he wanted to sleep.

He was allowed to rest for several days.

He slept and slept, and when he woke, he was in a room

high in the Institute's tall white-stone buildings. He shared it with Clair.

Below their window lay a high-walled garden with formal paths and a reflecting pond. Beyond the garden, the wild boy could see open country. But on all other sides, behind high walls, lay slate rooftops and city streets.

In the summer mornings, the sounds of carriages clattering over the cobblestones and the cries of street vendors would have drifted up from the streets below. And the city smells, too: chimney smoke and horse dung and a myriad others.

What would the wild boy's life be like in this place?

His door opened on a hallway that led to a spiral staircase. If he and Clair followed it, down and down, the marble steps led to the building's front doors, which opened on a courtyard walled by other school buildings and shaded by a giant elm. More doors, on the back side of the building, led to the garden that lay below the wild boy's window.

Everywhere, in the halls and on the spiral stairway and in the courtyard and gardens, children came and went. They never spoke aloud. Instead, they made gestures with their hands, the way the wild boy did.

When they played, they laughed and made natural, untrained cries, the way he did.

What did he think when he first saw these children who, like him, communicated with their hands and their eyes?

Perhaps in the beginning he watched them, closely, but they were not kind to him. He soon experienced what one observer described (without saying any more) as "a certain amount of ill-natured treatment" from "children of his own age."

What could the wild boy do then, but try to stay out of their way?

"He detests children of his own age and runs away from them without fail," wrote a man named J.-J. Virey. (Virey

was a scientist who worked at a nearby hospital, observed the wild boy at the Institute, and wrote a report on him.) "He likes solitude a great deal; crowds irritate him and make him uncomfortable and temperamental; he avoids them as much as possible." He also noted, "If he is afraid of something, he throws himself in the arms of his caretaker [Clair] and pushes him urgently toward his room, where he tries to close himself in and remain alone."

Already, a Paris vaudeville theater had staged a musical comedy called *The Savage of Aveyron.* A melodrama based on a novel about a wild child was showing at a second Paris theater.

A poster appeared with the caption "The Savage of Aveyron, currently at the Institute for Deaf-Mutes." It showed a drawing of a boy wearing a most peculiar costume: an orange-and-black striped gown with ruffles at the neck and sleeves, not to mention a ridiculous, beribboned hat.

And if that wasn't enough, the boy in the poster had what looked like claws on his hands and feet!

When sightseers got to the Institute, of course, they soon found out the poster was a fraud, but they kept coming anyway. The wild boy was "annoyed and victimized . . . by idle curiosity hunters of Paris," one man at the Institute for Deaf-Mutes wrote, "and by the so-called observers [scientists], who bothered him just as much."

The scientists, like all of Paris, were curious about the wild boy's past life. What was it *like*, they wondered, living in the forest like a wild beast?

The scientists were eager, too, to find the answers to questions that scientists in those days wondered about, such as "What is the True Nature of Man?" and "What role does Civilization play in the True Nature of Man?"

But for the wild boy to answer any of the scientists'

questions, he had to be taught to talk. And surely, the scientists thought, that wouldn't take long.

After all, the wild boy had a wonderful new teacher now: Abbé Sicard, the Miracle Worker.

A portrait of Abbé Sicard in his classroom shows a kindly man in a black coat, white wig, and shiny-buckled shoes. In the painting, he's trying to teach a young deaf girl to speak by holding her arm and applying a slight pressure to her wrist and elbow. Other girls, wearing elegant gowns and dainty slippers, watch with rapt attention.

It would indeed have been a miracle if such a method had worked, but it didn't. It is very, very difficult for truly deaf children to learn to speak aloud; pressing gently on their arms will not do the trick.

What the Institute for Deaf-Mutes actually did succeed in doing for its students was to teach them to read and write, using teachers who communicated with sign language. And that, in those days, was considered a "miracle."

But now, all of Paris expected the Abbé, the miracle worker, to do something he never had before: teach a "mute" child to talk.

And for some reason, Abbé Sicard did not seem eager to try.

Certainly the barefoot, dirty wild boy was not at all the kind of student the Abbé was used to: boys in uniforms, girls in white muslin dresses.

And besides, why should the Abbé risk his reputation by trying to teach some strange grubby boy who might be no more than an imbecile? What if the Abbé failed? *Then* what would people think of the "miracle worker"?

So as the days passed, the wild boy did not become Abbé Sicard's pupil after all. Instead, he remained only a spectacle exhibited to curious visitors.

At night, before the wild boy went to sleep, "he stood at the window, pressed against the grating, gazing at the countryside," J.-J. Virey wrote (after talking to Clair). "Sometimes he dreams and becomes agitated, as if he were vexed. He usually has these dreams after a lot of people have visited him during the day."

Was *this* to be his future?

One day at the end of August, the wild boy got into a carriage again, this time with Abbé Sicard and Professor Bonnaterre. It clattered through the Paris streets and stopped before a vast and splendid building. Soon, the wild boy was padding in his bare feet down gilded hallways and into the magnificent apartments of the French Minister of the Interior, Lucien Bonaparte.

The Minister had sent a letter to Abbé Sicard, telling him to present the "young savage of Aveyron" to him at noon that day.

One person who saw the wild boy there reported that the boy reminded him of a bear in a menagerie, his eyes glancing anxiously at the door and windows.

But the Minister of the Interior turned out to be an eccentric, artistic, and handsome young man. He patted the wild boy on the head and seemed well pleased with him, another observer wrote. The observer wrote, too, that the wild boy showed "lively joy."

The meeting lasted a little less than half an hour, but when it was over, the boy (though he would never know this) had made an important and influential friend.

After the meeting, the wild boy was let out in the Minister's garden, where (the first observer noticed) he ran very fast, giving "very lively cries of joy."

Fall came, and then the damp cold of a Paris winter. In the Institute's high-walled garden, the fruit trees pinned to the garden walls lost their leaves, the flowers withered, and the grass turned brown. The wild boy roamed the garden alone.

For Clair had gone home to Rodez.

The old man had once had a family of his own; in his lifetime, Clair was married and widowed twice. Now, perhaps, he had people who loved him waiting at home, but in any case, he had stayed with the wild boy as long as he could.

Before he left, Clair told the scientists that if they ever got tired of studying the wild boy, Clair would come back to Paris and get him. He'd take the wild boy home, Clair said, and be a father to him.

But the wild boy had no way of knowing that.

All he knew was that "his old guardian, whom he appears to love very much"—as one newspaper report had put it— was gone.

And now, the wild boy was neglected by everyone who

once had been so eager to bring him to Paris. Often, he went hungry. When he could get food from the kitchen, he crept in a corner and ate it all by himself. Sometimes, for reasons that were never written down, he was locked in a dark closet.

Sometimes he had seizures. He rocked back and forth endlessly. Deep in his throat, he made his unhappy humming noise.

Days went by, then weeks. And Clair did not come back.

The other children at the school — about forty boys and twenty girls — lived in a different world from the wild boy.

At five o'clock every morning, a drumroll so loud they could feel the vibrations woke the boys in their dormitory. They jumped from their cots, put on their uniforms of blue cotton blouses, blue pants, sweaters, and berets, and presented themselves for inspection. Then they trooped down the spiral staircase to the ground-floor dining hall.

After breakfast, the students went off to their classrooms, where they learned to read and write from their deaf tutors. The boys also worked in shops, where they learned trades such as carpentry, shoemaking, and tailoring.

After dinner, both boys and girls were let out to play in separate parts of the garden. When he saw the other children, the wild boy ran and hid.

Sometimes he crouched in the Institute's attic behind a pile of old building materials.

But when rain pattered on the roof and everyone else went inside, the wild boy often crept out into the garden, to the tiny, formal reflecting pond that sat among the flower beds. He would circle the pond several times, then sit by its edge and rock himself back and forth as the rain dimpled the surface of the pond. He'd gaze into the water, toss in a handful of dead leaves, and watch them drift.

·VIII·

The child with whom I have been concerned is not, as is generally believed, a hopeless imbecile but an interesting being.

—Jean-Marc-Gaspard Itard, *The Wild Boy of Aveyron*

THE RAIN FELL STEADILY.

Inside the Institute a young doctor stood at the window, looking out into the garden. Like the wild boy, he had dark, deep-set eyes and unruly hair. His name was Jean-Marc-Gaspard Itard.

He worked in the hospital just down the street, and sometimes he came to the Institute to treat the students there.

Some time ago, he had noticed the strange boy roaming the Institute garden. He had begun observing him, quietly and from a distance. He had noticed the wild boy's habit of sitting alone by the pond in the rain. "I have often stopped for hours with inexpressible delight to consider him in this situation," he wrote later. But Dr. Itard was not the only one watching the wild boy.

That winter, a famous psychiatrist named Philippe Pinel issued a report that, like Professor Bonnaterre's, concluded that the wild boy was most likely an "imbecile." The report went on to suggest that if the boy really *was* an imbecile, then the best place for him was . . . *an insane asylum.*

Pinel himself had been the director of two Paris insane asylums: one for men and boys, and one for women and girls. He believed "imbecile" children must be "condemned to vegetate sadly in our asylums" because they were incapable of learning.

The asylum where boys were sent was called Bicêtre. It was a huge, fortress-like building on a hill just south of Paris.

Only a few years earlier, it had been a terrible prison.

"Debtors are incarcerated [imprisoned] here," a man called Louis-Sébastien Mercier wrote of Bicêtre. "Beggars, and madmen, together with all the viler criminals, huddled pell-mell. There are others, too; epileptics, imbeciles. . . ."

Mercier described Bicêtre's "subterranean dungeons, cut off from the light of day and the sounds of the outer world, save for a couple of tiny outlets in the roof."

The wild boy, fortunately for him, had no way of knowing what awaited him if people listened to the famous Dr. Pinel.

But the young, unknown doctor who had been watching the wild boy with such pleasure did.

And Dr. Itard believed it was *wrong* to send the wild boy to Bicêtre. Society had no right, he wrote, "to tear a child away from a free and innocent life, and send him to die of boredom in an institution."

"I never shared this unfavorable opinion," he wrote of Pinel's report. Dr. Itard believed the wild boy *could* be taught. "I dared to conceive certain hopes."

So Dr. Itard went to Abbé Sicard and asked for permission to become the wild boy's teacher. Abbé Sicard granted that, and more. He gave Dr. Itard a job as the resident doctor at the Institute for Deaf-Mutes, and with it, an apartment on the Institute's fourth floor, high above the garden. There, the young doctor could spend all the time he wanted on the task no one else would take — the education of a dirty wild boy.

I believed that there was a simpler and above all, more humane method, namely, to treat him kindly and to exercise great consideration for his tastes and inclinations.

—Jean-Marc-Gaspard Itard, *The Wild Boy of Aveyron*

WHEN THE REFLECTING POND was skimmed with ice and gray skies hung low over Paris, the wild boy had a fire to sit by. He could watch the flames in peace, with no one to tell him "for shame." He could sit drowsily in a corner, his stomach full, safe from cold-eyed scientists and whispering, giggling sightseers. The wild boy had a new home.

He had gone to live with Dr. Itard's housekeeper, Madame Guérin, who lived at the Institute with her husband, Monsieur Guérin. Madame Guérin, Dr. Itard wrote later, was a person with "all the patience of a mother and the intelligence of an enlightened teacher."

The wild boy had his own room, just down the hall from Dr. Itard's study.

Although the wild boy didn't know it, Madame Guérin and Dr. Itard had a plan for him. In the beginning, it was quite simple: to treat him kindly, give him plenty of food, and let him do whatever he wanted.

"It was necessary," Dr. Itard wrote later, "to make him happy in his own way."

Every day, the wild boy had a long, hot bath, and after a while, he began to lose his animal-like ability to withstand cold. When it was time for him to get in the water, he would test it with his fingers to see if it was warm enough. One time when it wasn't, he grabbed Madame Guérin's hand and stuck it in to show her.

Now that he felt the cold, the wild boy began to be less impatient about wearing clothing. He'd realized, Itard wrote, that clothes kept him warm. One chilly morning when the wild boy woke up, someone had left his clothes right by his bed. After several mornings, the wild boy put them on himself. In time — although he disliked them most of all and they always made his gait a little heavy — he even wore shoes.

It was all part of Dr. Itard's plan.

Every day, the boy was allowed to do what he liked, and for now that meant the things he knew best: "sleeping, eating, doing nothing and running about the fields."

Almost every day, Dr. Itard or Madame Guérin took him for a walk. They went either to the garden of the Paris Observatory or to the Luxembourg Gardens. Both were only a few blocks from the Institute for Deaf-Mutes.

Not that the wild boy walked. They walked, but he trotted, loped, or galloped. As Dr. Itard put it, these outings were not so much walks as "scampers." Often, the wild boy would

stop to sniff things that to Dr. Itard seemed to have no smell. It was as though the wild boy could sense a whole different world, the world that dogs understand, where smells tell an invisible story. "I have many times seen him stop, and even turn round, to pick up pebbles and bits of dried wood, which he threw away only after holding them to his nose, often with the appearance of great satisfaction," Itard wrote.

The wild boy's new life, wrote Dr. Itard, "was the beginning of the intense affection which he has acquired for his governess [Madame Guérin] and which he sometimes expresses in a most touching manner. He never leaves her without reluctance nor does he rejoin her without signs of satisfaction."

Dr. Itard was a serious, studious man who stayed a bachelor all his life. But even he realized how important it was for the wild boy to have a mother. Itard wrote about it in his own, sometimes rather hard-to-understand way, like this: "I shall perhaps be understood if my readers will remember the . . . influence exerted upon a child's mind by the inexhaustible delights and the maternal triflings that nature has put into the heart of a mother and which make the first smiles flower and bring to birth life's earliest joys."

What he meant was: children need mothers, and now that the wild boy had one, he could begin to be happy.

It didn't take much, really. "A ray of sun reflected upon a mirror in his room and turning about on the ceiling, a glass of water let fall drop by drop from a certain height upon his fingertips while he was in the bath, and a wooden porringer containing a little milk placed at the end of his bath, which the . . . [waves] of the water drifted, little by little, amid cries of delight, into his grasp," Dr. Itard wrote. "Such simple means were nearly all that was necessary to divert and delight this child of nature."

Once when it snowed heavily during the night, the wild boy woke up and with "a cry of joy" ran half-dressed into the garden, Itard wrote. "There, giving vent to his delight by the most piercing cries, he ran, rolled himself in the snow and gathered it by handfuls, feasting on it with incredible eagerness."

As part of his plan to make the wild boy happy, Dr. Itard often took the boy with him when he was invited out to dinner. If they went on foot, it was impossible to make the wild boy walk by Itard's side; the boy always wanted to trot or gallop ahead. So instead of walking, they rode in a carriage.

The carriage would rattle through the narrow streets, past tall houses all joined together and capped with shallow roofs like flat-topped hats, so common in Paris. They'd pass archways leading to cobbled courtyards, or poor neighborhoods where ragpickers and water carriers hurried down the streets, going home to their attic rooms. As it got dark, men would light the oil lamps that hung from ropes strung from one side of the street to the other.

The carriage would stop in front of a house glowing with candle- and lantern light.

Inside, the table would be set with the wild boy's favorite dishes. He would make sounds to the hostess, asking her for what he wanted. If she pretended not to hear him, he'd put his plate beside the dish and stare at it longingly, then rap on his plate with a fork. And if *that* didn't work, he could wait no longer. *Whoosh!* He'd empty the dish onto his plate with a spoon or even his hand.

The wild boy always knew when they were going out to eat, because Dr. Itard would appear in the late afternoon wearing his hat and carrying a clean, folded shirt. The boy would change into it as fast as he could, then follow Itard out the door.

Itard had a name for his pupil now. He called him Victor.

Victor. It had a nice ring to it. A *victor*—a winner—is someone who triumphs over all obstacles.

Dr. Itard wrote that he chose it for the wild boy's name because in French, the name Victor has an "oh" sound in it—it's pronounced "veek-tOHr"—and Dr. Itard had noticed that the wild boy seemed to turn his head when he heard people say the sound "oh."

But Dr. Itard may have had another reason, too, for choosing *Victor*—the hope that someday, the wild boy would live up to his new name.

· X ·

. . . in moments of great happiness.

—Jean-Marc-Gaspard Itard, *The Wild Boy of Aveyron*

EVERY MORNING, Victor would have breakfast with Madame Guérin and her husband, Monsieur Guérin. Every day, he would set the table with three places. Often, she'd send him down to the Institute's kitchen to bring back food for their meals.

He'd trot down the hall. Then, when he got to the marble staircase leading to the first floor, where the kitchen was, he'd listen carefully. If he heard echoing footsteps and the laughter of other students, he would stay back until he was sure to avoid them.

Victor liked the neatness and order of the Guérins' apartment. When something was left out of its proper place, he'd put it back.

Sometimes he went down the hall to Dr. Itard's study and sat on the sofa.

From time to time, curious visitors came to the apartment. But now if Victor decided they'd stayed too long, he would present them with their hats, gloves, and walking canes, push them gently out the door, and shut it firmly behind them.

Each day, he seemed to grow more like other people. He dressed neatly, in a gentleman's waistcoat like Dr. Itard's. A person who didn't know Victor might even mistake him for "an almost ordinary child who cannot speak," Itard wrote proudly.

In the evenings, after Victor had gone to bed, Dr. Itard would sometimes stop by to say good night. Victor would sit up for a hug, then pull him close, until Dr. Itard was sitting next to him on the bed. The boy would take Dr. Itard's hand and put it on his own head — his eyes, his forehead, his hair — and let it rest there for a long time.

Sometimes Victor would pat the knees of Dr. Itard's velvet pants, rubbing the fuzz this way and that and then, sometimes, putting his lips two or three times to Itard's velvet knees.

At times like these, Dr. Itard was not a teacher, but as close to a father as he knew how to be. "People may say what they like," Dr. Itard wrote, "but I will confess that I lend myself without ceremony to all this childish play."

The wild boy's new family also included Madame Guérin's husband, Monsieur Guérin, but very little is known about him.

And there was still one more member, an even more mysterious figure: a girl named Julie. She was eleven or twelve years old, just about Victor's age.

She was Madame Guérin's daughter.

For some reason no one knows, she didn't live in the apartment with Monsieur and Madame Guérin. But on Sundays, she came to visit. And in time, Madame Guérin began to notice that when Julie came, the boy made a sound that no one had ever taught him.

"Lee!" he'd say happily. "Lee! Lee! Lee!"

In the middle of the night, when Madame Guérin thought Victor was asleep, she would hear him calling all by himself in his room. "Lee! Lee! Lee!"

"He is often heard to repeat *lli lli* [lee! lee!] with an

inflection of voice not without sweetness," Dr. Itard wrote. "I am somewhat inclined to believe that in this painful linguistic labor there is a sort of feeling after the name of Julie."

It must have been odd for Julie to have a boy who had once lived all by himself in the forest for a brother, but she does not seem to have minded.

If she had stared at him with distaste, Victor (who was good at reading faces) would have known right away. And surely, he would have avoided her, or brought her bonnet and shawl and tried to hurry her out the door.

But instead, he called out her name.

No one can know whether he and Julie really became friends, but there's a story from around this time (about another, equally mysterious girl) that offers a tiny clue.

Once, a person watching the wild boy on his trips to the Observatory Gardens with Madame Guérin noticed that Victor seemed to be fond of a young girl, the daughter of an astronomer. Sometimes she would motion to him to sit next

to her, and he would obey very shyly, like a puppy with his master. If something distracted him, though, he'd run away.

The story seems to show that sometimes, Victor *did* make friends with children his own age.

So maybe Julie was his friend, too.

Dr. Itard wrote very little about the wild boy's life with the Guérin family, but one thing is certain: when he was with them, he began, all on his own, to say the beginnings of words.

Victor often heard Madame Guérin use the expression *"Oh Dieu!"* (*Dieu*, pronounced "dyuh," is the French word for "God") and after a while, he began to imitate her. "Oh dee!" he'd cry. "Oh dee! Oh dee!"

He said it often, Dr. Itard noticed, "in moments of great happiness."

Everything put the faculties of the intelligence into play and
prepared them for the great work of the communication of ideas.

—Jean-Marc-Gaspard Itard, *The Wild Boy of Aveyron*

IN TIME, Victor's life of doing whatever he wanted all day long came to an end. It began with toys.

"I have . . . shown him toys of all kinds; more than once I have tried for whole hours to teach him how to use them," Dr. Itard wrote, "and I have seen with sorrow that, far from attracting his attention, [they] always ended by making him so impatient that he came to the point of hiding them or destroying them. . . . Thus, one day when he was alone in his room he took upon himself to throw into the fire a game of ninepins with which we had pestered him. . . . [We found him] gaily warming himself before his bonfire."

But Dr. Itard—unlike Victor—was a very patient person. If one thing didn't work, he tried another. After dinner one night, he took some silver cups and turned them upside down on the table. He put a chestnut underneath one of the cups. Victor watched, curious.

The game was an old carnival trick: the one in which a person hides something under one of several cups, then moves them around to see if the person watching can still find the cup with the hidden object.

Victor could.

When Itard replaced the nuts with things that weren't food, Victor still wanted to play the game.

Dr. Itard was pleased. He wrote that the game was a good

mental exercise for Victor; it helped develop his attention span and judgment. It taught him to fix his restless eyes in one place.

One day, when Victor was very thirsty, Dr. Itard offered him a glass of water and said, *"Eau! Eau!"* (*Eau*, pronounced "oh," is the French word for "water.") And then . . . Dr. Itard wouldn't give him the water.

Victor waved his hands near the glass, but Dr. Itard acted as though he didn't understand.

Madame Guérin stood watching. *"Eau!"* said Madame Guérin, and Dr. Itard gave the glass of water to her, just like that.

"Eau!" said Itard. *"Eau!"* And Madame Guérin gave the water back.

Victor was frantic. "Water!" he gestured. "Water!" But, Dr. Itard and Madame Guérin acted as though they didn't understand!

Victor's arms were flailing, almost as though he were

having a seizure, when Dr. Itard finally gave him the water. "It would have been inhuman to insist further," Itard wrote later.

The next day when Victor sat down to breakfast and held out his cup for milk, Dr. Itard said, *"Lait!"* (pronounced "lay," which in French means "milk"). *Lait.* He looked at Victor. *"Lait!"* he said again.

Victor was silent.

It happened the next day, too. Victor held out his cup for milk, and Dr. Itard just looked at him. *"Lait!"* said Dr. Itard, but Victor didn't respond.

On the fourth day, Victor held out his cup for milk. As it poured into his cup, he said something very softly, almost under his breath.

"Lait," he said. Then he repeated it. *"Lait."*

Dr. Itard was pleased, but he wasn't satisfied.

Victor hadn't said the word *before* he'd gotten the milk.

He'd still asked for milk in his old way, by holding out his cup, but Dr. Itard wanted Victor to ask for milk, with a word, not a gesture.

Now every time Victor wanted milk and held out his cup, Dr. Itard would stall, hoping Victor would ask for it in words.

But Victor had his *own* way of asking — by holding out his cup.

Only when, "despairing of success," Dr. Itard had given Victor his milk would he say anything.

"*Lait,*" Victor would say happily, as the milk poured into his cup. "*Lait!*"

Victor had no way of knowing it, of course, but after that, Dr. Itard devised another plan: if Victor wouldn't *say* words to ask for things, maybe he could learn to ask with *written* words. Itard hoped to teach him bit by bit, in little, tiny steps.

So one day when Dr. Itard came to Victor's room, he brought a blackboard and chalk. First he drew outlines on it: a key, scissors, and a hammer. Then he set a real key, scissors, and hammer on the blackboard, each object on top of its outline. Next, he picked up all the objects and took them to another room.

Back at the blackboard, he pointed to an outline to show what he wanted, then motioned to Victor to bring that thing. One by one, Victor had to go to the other room and fetch whatever Itard wanted. After a while, to save himself the trouble of trotting back and forth, Victor just brought everything at once, but Dr. Itard didn't like that.

So Dr. Itard tried keeping all the objects in the same room as the chalkboard. All Victor had to do was pick each one up and place it on its correct outline. It wasn't hard, and Victor was successful at matching objects to outlines.

After a while, Dr. Itard brought many more objects and drew their outlines on the board. Victor looked at each one, searched for its outline on the blackboard, then placed it where it belonged.

So then Dr. Itard made the exercises harder. He brought in a variety of cardboard shapes in a variety of colors, for Victor to match up in pairs. To match them, Victor had to tell the difference not just between a circle and a square but also between a square and a slightly flattened square, and not just between red and blue but also between sky blue and gray blue, and so on. Each day, the shapes became more complicated and difficult. If Victor made a mistake or was uncertain, Dr. Itard made him do the task over and over and over.

One day, Victor threw all the cardboard pieces on the floor and stomped off toward his bed.

Dr. Itard made him pick up the shapes and match them.

The next day, there were more shapes; the day after that, more. . . .

Sometimes Victor ran to his bed and bit the sheets and blanket. He attacked the fireplace, scattering ashes and red-hot coals and tossing aside the iron frames that held the logs.

One day he got so angry, it seemed as though he were having a seizure.

But every day, there were more cards, and more shapes.

Then one day when Victor went into a fit of anger, Dr. Itard remembered something that had happened some time earlier, when Victor and Madame Guérin had gone to the Observatory Gardens.

That day, they had climbed the spiral stairs inside the Observatory and emerged on the rooftop observation platform. Victor went to the railing to look out and was seized with fright. Itard described it later: "Trembling in every limb and his face covered with sweat, he returned to his governess, whom he dragged by the arm towards the door."

Now, remembering Victor's fear of heights, Itard strode to the room's fourth-story window and threw it open. "With every appearance of anger," Dr. Itard wrote, he advanced upon

Victor, grabbed him by the seat of his pants, and thrust him out the window with his head hanging over the stone courtyard, far below. He let Victor dangle, "his head directly turned towards the bottom of the chasm."

Then, at last, he pulled Victor back in.

"He was pale, covered with a cold sweat, his eyes were rather tearful, and he still trembled a little," Dr. Itard wrote later. "I led him to his cards. I made him gather them up and replace them all. . . . Afterwards he went and threw himself on his bed and wept."

It was the first time Dr. Itard had ever seen him cry.

From then on, when Dr. Itard made Victor do his lessons even when he was tired or it was time to go outside. Victor no longer went into rages. He "contented himself with giving signs of weariness and impatience, and uttering a plaintive murmur which ordinarily ended in tears."

But after that day, Victor did something that his teacher wrote only a few lines about—he ran away.

Dr. Itard wrote that Victor "escaped" from Madame Guérin on the streets and "shed many tears on seeing her again." Hours later, his breath still came in gasps and his heart was racing fast.

Another time, he went out wandering on a wide street crowded with carriages, called the rue d'Enfer. Night had fallen before Madame Guérin found him. He recognized her in the dark by the smell of her hands and arms and was so happy he laughed out loud.

· XII ·

*The child known under the name of the Savage of Aveyron is
endowed with the free use of all his senses. . . . His education
is possible, if it is not already guaranteed, by this early success.*

—Jean-Marc-Gaspard Itard, *The Wild Boy of Aveyron*

EACH DAY when Victor's lessons were over, he could go
outside with Madame Guerin.

When the hour neared for their trip to the park, he'd drift
to the window. He'd hover at the door. When it took Madame
Guérin too long to get ready, he'd get her bonnet and shawl
and set them in front of her. Sometimes he was so impatient,

he'd try to put them on her himself. Then he'd open the door, lifting the latch (by pulling the latch string) himself.

When they went to the gardens that lay around the Paris observatory, Madame Guérin and Victor would often visit the Observatory's caretaker, who had a house on the grounds.

The man always gave Victor a drink of milk in a china cup. One day by accident, Victor broke the cup. So the next day, all on his own, he brought a little wooden bowl. After that he always brought the bowl in his pocket.

After his milk, he liked to get people to give him rides in a wheelbarrow. He'd find someone in the caretaker's house, take the person by the arm, lead them to the wheelbarrow, and climb in. If the person didn't push him right away, he'd get out and roll the wheelbarrow a little way himself, to make sure they understood. Then he'd get in again and wait for his ride.

One day, Madame Guérin brought Victor a set of metal

squares. They fit neatly into a specially made box that had rows of little wooden compartments, each one marked.

The mark on the first compartment looked like this: *A.*

The mark on the last one looked like this: *Z.*

It was Victor's task to take all the metal squares out, then put each one back into the compartment where the mark matched the shape. *A . . . B . . . C . . .*

So Victor took them all out, in order, and set them aside in neat stacks, in order. Then, without ever having to look at the shapes themselves, he set them all back in the right place. *Bang, bang, bang,* and it was done!

Dr. Itard came in and watched.

After that, Dr. Itard made Madame Guérin mix all the shapes up. *Then* Victor had to put them all back, each in the right compartment.

Dr. Itard's way was a lot more trouble, but Victor did it anyhow.

One morning at breakfast time, Dr. Itard arrived, bringing a board and four metal shapes.

Dr. Itard put the shapes on the board and pointed to them.

L-A-I-T.

Then Madame Guérin gave Dr. Itard some milk.

Dr. Itard held the milk pitcher in one hand and gave the letters to Victor with the other.

Victor put the letters back on the board like this:

T-A-I-L.

That didn't seem to be what his teacher wanted. So he tried again.

L-A-I-T.

Both Dr. Itard and Madame Guérin seemed very pleased! Beaming, Madame Guérin poured the milk into his cup.

A week later, when it was time for his walk with Madame Guérin to the Observatory Gardens, Victor brought along his little wooden bowl, the same as he always did. But, unknown to anyone, he had also brought something else.

When they got to the house where he was always given milk, he reached into his pocket, took out four metal shapes, and laid them on the table.

L-A-I-T.

·XIII·

There is always the same passion for the country, the same ecstasy
at the sight of a beautiful bright moon or a field covered with
snow, and the same . . . [joy] at the noise of a stormy wind.

—Jean-Marc-Gaspard Itard, *The Wild Boy of Aveyron*

VICTOR COULD TELL when his teacher was happy.

And now, he'd made his teacher very, *very* happy.

But there was something deep inside Victor that still
longed for his old life.

One night when the full moon shone through his window,
Victor woke and stood looking out, past the formal gardens
and over the Institute walls to where the moonlit fields began.

Downstairs, Madame Guérin heard his footsteps and went quietly up to his room to see what was happening. Victor stood by the window, his forehead close to the glass, his eyes fixed on the distant fields. Now and then, he drew deep breaths and made a sad little sound.

Madame Guérin noticed it happened often when the moon was full.

Only once since he'd come to Paris had Victor been allowed outside the city. He and Itard had driven to the countryside north of Paris, where Dr. Itard was visiting some friends. In the carriage, Victor stared eagerly out one window and then another, his joy showing in his eyes and his whole body. Whenever the horses slowed and seemed about to stop, his excitement grew.

When he and Itard reached the country house, "such was the effect of these outside influences, of these woods, these hills, with which he could never satisfy his eyes, that he appeared more impatient and wild than ever," Itard wrote. The boy could scarcely eat: he seemed to Itard to be wishing he were back in his old life, "an independent life, happy and regretted."

After that, Dr. Itard decided the country was too much of a temptation for Victor. Instead, he would be allowed to go only to formal gardens like the Luxembourg. There, the flowers were planted in squares, the trees grew in rows, and the fountains sat at the ends of straight paths. The gardens' "straight and regular arrangement had nothing in common with the great landscapes of which wild nature is composed," Dr. Itard wrote. They were nature civilized. Nature tamed.

Once, in the summertime, Victor and Dr. Itard were invited to dinner at the grand country house of an elegant, beautiful, very fashionable lady named Jeanne Françoise Julie Adélaïde Récamier. Madame Récamier, who was known for her glittering parties, thought that meeting the famous wild boy would amuse her other dinner guests. She'd invited a general, an ambassador, a number of French aristocrats, an English lord and his lady, two duchesses, and the future king of Sweden and Norway.

Dr. Itard and Victor arrived in a carriage. Victor hopped out.

Inside Madame Récamier's château, the summer light shone through windows hung with silk draperies. Room after room was decorated with dark mahogany furniture, bronze candleholders, and marble statues. Madame Récamier's couch, built in the style of the lost city of Pompeii, sat beneath a "garland of flowers, escaping from the beaks of two gilt-bronze swans." Such couches were all the rage that year.

When they reached the dining room, "Madame Récamier seated him at her side, thinking perhaps that the same beauty that had captivated civilized man would receive similar homage from this child of nature," Madame Récamier's biographer wrote. But "the young savage hardly heeded the beautiful

eyes whose attention he had himself attracted." Instead, the wild boy ate his dinner with "startling greed," filled his pockets with "all the delicacies that he could filch," and left the table.

Absorbed in their dinner-table discussions, none of the guests, it was said, even noticed Victor was gone until they heard a noise from the garden. They rushed outside to see the boy "running across the lawn with the speed of a rabbit," dressed only in his undershirt. Then, the story goes, he ripped it off and jumped naked from tree to tree till he was lured down with a basket of peaches, . . . wrapped in a petticoat belonging to the gardener's niece, and sent home.

The Savage of Aveyron was "bundled into the carriage that brought him," one horrified observer reported, "leaving the guests at Clichy-la-Garenne to draw a sweeping and useful comparison between the perfection of the civilized life and the distressing picture of nature untamed."

Madame Récamier and her guests trailed back into the

château. That evening, they ate fruit and ices and played charades.

The Distressing Picture of Nature Untamed (along with, perhaps, the basket of peaches) was soon back in the city, at home with Dr. Itard and Madame and Monsieur Guérin.

And with Julie, too, on Sundays.

XIV

I was obliged to reply to the everlasting objections. "Does the Savage speak? If he is not deaf why does he not speak?"

—Jean-Marc-Gaspard Itard, *The Wild Boy of Aveyron*

ONE TIME, during a lesson, Victor noticed that Dr. Itard was using a little metal tool to hold a piece of chalk too short to pick up with his fingers. When Victor was alone in his room, he decided to make his own chalk holder. He rummaged in a cupboard, found an old kitchen skewer, and tied a piece of chalk to it with thread.

A few days later, Dr. Itard found the tool in Victor's room.

By the "inspiration of really creative imagination," he was clever enough to convert the kitchen skewer into a real chalk holder, Dr. Itard wrote, thrilled. It was the kind of thing that gave the doctor hope that someday, his pupil would learn to talk.

Dr. Itard had always dreamed that if Victor could learn what words were really *for,* the two of them would be able to communicate mind to mind, and "the most rapid progress would spring from this first triumph."

But no matter how hard Dr. Itard tried, Victor didn't seem to understand that words were the only real way to communicate.

But was that really true? *Were* words the only real way to communicate?

Each day when the students at the Institute for Deaf-Mutes walked from their classes to their workshops or streamed out into the garden to play, they laughed and chattered among themselves. But they didn't chatter out loud.

As their heads bent toward one another, their fingers danced in intricate patterns as fast as speech. Ideas flew through the air. With their hands and eyes and faces, they could talk about their lives before they came to the Institute and their hopes for the future. They could discuss God and the universe. Each morning, they said the Lord's Prayer in sign language.

Dr. Itard had known from the first time he'd met the wild boy that communicating with hand gestures came naturally to him.

Yet it never seemed to occur to Dr. Itard to try to teach Victor formal sign language.

Dr. Itard himself had never learned it, even though he spent more than thirty years working at a school for deaf children. Like many people in those days, he did not believe that the formal signing used by deaf people was a real language. He wanted Victor to *speak*, and to Itard, that meant speaking aloud.

• • •

As the months went by, Dr. Itard devised one lesson after another. Victor had no way of knowing that every single one of them had the same goal: that someday, *someday,* he would learn to talk.

Victor learned to read a few words, yet "this reading conveyed no meaning to him," Dr. Itard wrote sadly.

Dr. Itard made labels: BOOK and SCISSORS and HAMMER. He showed Victor the labels, then told him to get what was on them. Back and forth Victor would go, from his room to Dr. Itard's study. "He often stopped in the corridor, put his face to the window which is at one end of it, greeted with sharp cries the sight of the country which unfolds magnificently in the distance, and then set off again for his room, got his little cargo, renewed his homage to the ever-regretted beauties of nature, and returned to me quite sure of the correctness of his errand," Itard wrote.

121

When Victor did well at his lessons and his teacher praised him, happiness would spread across his face. He'd laugh out loud. But other times, when he didn't understand, he'd become deeply unhappy. "I have seen him moisten with his tears the characters which are so unintelligible to him, although he has not been provoked by any word of reproach, threat, or punishment," Itard wrote.

And still, the lessons went on.

Dr. Itard blindfolded Victor and had him listen to different sounds: a bell, a drum, a wind instrument, even the ringing of a rod struck upon a fire shovel. Victor liked these lessons — he used to bring the blindfold to Dr. Itard and "stamp with joy when he felt my hands tie it firmly behind his head."

Dr. Itard said the sounds of the vowels ("Oh! Oh!") and had Victor raise a different finger for each of the letters *a, e, i, o,* and *u.*

Dr. Itard had Victor watch his teacher's face and imitate the expressions he made. "Thus we have instructor and

pupil facing each other and grimacing their hardest." After that, Dr. Itard had Victor try to imitate his voice when he talked. But the sounds Victor made now were less like talking than they had been, long ago, when the lessons first began.

Once, on a day when Victor's lessons had gone particularly badly, Dr. Itard sat down in despair. He recalled it later in his writings.

"'Unhappy creature,' I cried as if he could hear me, and with real anguish of heart, 'since my labors are wasted and your efforts fruitless, take again the road to your forests and the taste for your primitive life. Or . . . go . . . die of misery and boredom at Bicêtre.'

"Scarcely had I finished speaking," Dr. Itard wrote, "when I saw his chest heave noisily, his eyes shut, and a stream of tears escape through his closed eyelids, with him the signs of bitter grief."

Itard wrote that at times he wished he'd never met the wild boy. Sometimes he wondered whether it had been right, so long ago, to tear the boy from his old, happy life in the forest and bring him to live in Paris.

But now, of course, it was too late.

XV

To speak of the Wild Boy of Aveyron is to revive a name which now no longer arouses any kind of interest; it is to recall a creature forgotten by those who merely saw him and disdained by those who have thought to pass judgment on him.

—Jean-Marc-Gaspard Itard, *The Wild Boy of Aveyron*

WITHIN THE HIGH WALLS of the Institute for Deaf-Mutes, the boy who was called Victor grew into a young man of about eighteen.

Then, one day in June of 1806, a letter arrived at the Institute, addressed to Dr. Itard. It was from the French Minister of the Interior, an office now held not by Lucien

Bonaparte, the wild boy's eccentric friend, but by one of his successors, Jean-Baptiste de Champagny. "I know, sir, that your care of the young Victor who was entrusted to you five years ago has been as generous as it has been diligent," the Minister wrote.

For all those years, ever since Lucien Bonaparte first authorized it, the government had been sending money to the Institute for Deaf-Mutes to pay for Victor's education. Now, the current Minister wrote, it was "essential for humanity and for science to know the results."

And what could Dr. Itard say?

He would have to tell the Minister that Victor had not learned to speak.

The experiment Dr. Itard had begun with such "brilliant hopes" had ended in failure. And it was not just Victor's failure, but Dr. Itard's as well. He claimed that for himself, he didn't care. "As for me," he wrote, "I am quite indifferent both to forgetfulness and to disdain."

There would be no more lessons.

Dr. Itard wrote that he had decided to resign himself to failure and abandon his pupil to "incurable dumbness."

At about that same time, Madame Guérin's husband, Monsieur Guérin, fell ill. For years, he had sat down every day to meals with Victor and Madame Guérin, but now he was taken away from the apartment to be nursed back to health. Victor didn't know that, so he kept setting Monsieur Guérin's place at the table, only to be told to put it away. Then finally, Monsieur Guérin died.

That evening Victor set Monsieur Guérin's place. When she saw it, Madame Guérin burst into tears.

Victor put Monsieur Guérin's dishes back in the cupboard and never set his place again.

Then Madame Guérin herself got sick. For days, she lay in bed. The hour for Victor's walks came and went, but he waited patiently. Two weeks passed, and at last, Madame Guérin was able to get up again.

"As soon as his governess [Madame Guérin] left her sick bed, his happiness burst forth, and became greater still when, on a very beautiful day, he saw her prepare to go out," Itard wrote. Madame Guérin put on her bonnet and shawl . . . but she left the apartment alone.

When she returned, she sent Victor to the kitchen to fetch their supper. He loped down the stairway and into the courtyard.

Just then, on the busy streets on the other side of the wall, a carriage rattled and came to a stop. The gatekeeper swung open the heavy wooden doors, and the carriage drove into the courtyard.

In the instant before the gates closed again, Victor slipped through and was gone.

XVI

Hurrying into the street, [he] rapidly gained the Barrière d'Enfer.

—Jean-Marc-Gaspard Itard, *The Wild Boy of Aveyron*

A CLOSE OBSERVER might have noticed something odd about the silent, neatly dressed young man hurrying down the street called the rue d'Enfer. His gait, perhaps, was a little heavy. But soon, Victor was just one more figure in the crowds on the busy streets.

He hurried past the Luxembourg Gardens, where he'd once scampered with Dr. Itard. He passed the Observatory Gardens, where he'd gone for his walks with Madame Guérin and been taken, years ago, for rides in a wheelbarrow. What did that matter now?

At the end of the rue d'Enfer stood a massive stone gate known as the Barrière d'Enfer, one of many gates set in the wall that encircled the city of Paris. It was guarded by men in stiff blue-and-red coats and shiny boots.

Perhaps Victor stopped there and gazed uneasily, remembering the policemen who had once taken him by horseback to the orphanage. Perhaps he turned away from the gate. But in any case, he was not caught.

Days went by, and no one had any idea where Victor was. Perhaps Madame Guérin and Dr. Itard asked people in the neighborhood if they'd seen him. Maybe they went by carriage from police station to police station, asking if he'd been picked up. But beyond that, there was little they could do but wait for news that might—or might not—come.

Victor was free now. He was on his own.

The city all around him held many places to hide, for in those days, inside the walls of Paris, many leafy, sheltering places still remained. "From my window on the rue d'Enfer," wrote one man, a playwright remembering Paris then, "I used to cast my eyes, as far as I could see in every direction, over a wealth of foliage."

Behind the houses that lined many of the streets of Paris lay tree-shaded courtyards and sunny gardens separated only by low fences. In some parts of the city, not far from the Institute for Deaf-Mutes, it was almost like being in the country.

"Along all the left bank of the river [Seine]," the man wrote, "there were only scattered dwellings amidst orchards, kitchen-gardens, trellis-vineyards, farmyards, groves, and parks planted with century-old trees."

Surely Victor would have preferred quiet, leafy places. It's possible he worked his way from one green, wild place to the next, searching for a way past the city walls. But whether he went by busy streets or quiet ones, Victor headed north.

When he came to the river Seine, perhaps he stopped to look at brightly painted laundry boats where women washed clothes in the water and hung them, flapping, on lines in the breeze. Maybe he watched as men with poles guided long, narrow barges downstream.

A stone bridge, the Pont de la Tournelle, arched over the river to an island in the Seine. To reach the island, Victor would have joined a stream of carriages, carts, animals, and people on foot swarming across the bridge.

Just upstream, on another island, rose the famous cathedral of Notre Dame, with its two great stone towers, taller even than the cathedral of Rodez.

A second bridge, and Victor would have crossed the Seine to the narrow, crowded streets on the other side.

When night came, he had to find a place to sleep. Perhaps he bedded down in the straw in one of the horse stables that could be found throughout the city, for runaways often took shelter there. Maybe he slept on the streets, but in any case, no one seems to have noticed him, as no news of his whereabouts reached Madame Guérin or Dr. Itard. All alone, he made his way through a city of half a million people.

Somehow, after starting from the Barrière d'Enfer on the very southern and western end of Paris, he managed to travel all the way to the other end of the city, to its far northeast edge. And somehow, by a means known only to himself, Victor passed through the city gates to the open country beyond.

·**XVII**·

He turned in the direction of Senlis and gained the forest.

—Jean-Marc-Gaspard Itard, *The Wild Boy of Aveyron*

THE ROADS THAT LED OUT OF PARIS were wide
and smoothly paved, passing through countryside dotted with
villages. After a time—perhaps one day, perhaps several days
and nights—Victor reached a forest named after a village
called Senlis.

The road that ran through it was perfectly straight, for it happened that the forest of Senlis had once been the king's hunting preserve. It was pierced through with roads, built so that the king and his horsemen could chase their prey with ease. In places, many roads came together; signposts bristled with arrows pointing in all directions.

So no matter how far into the trees Victor ventured, he couldn't avoid roads. And even if he *could* find a hiding place in those woods, then what?

At night, there was no fire to warm him, no light but the stars and the cold, distant moon. When he was hungry, he could search for bitter acorns or raw chestnuts, but he'd never find a warm meal or sit at a table with people who cared about him.

Perhaps now he also felt a different kind of hunger: a kind of loneliness he never knew in his old, wild days.

If he had a home in the world, it wasn't here.

He left the forest and made his way back across the open fields.

By the time he came out of the woods, Victor's clothes were muddy and torn. The next thing he knew, the police had mistaken him for a vagabond and arrested him.

They threw him into a country jail, perhaps into a dark cell with only a shred of sky glimpsed through a barred window. Day after day he languished there. Two weeks passed before, by some lucky chance, someone realized who he was: the strange, wild Savage of Aveyron.

He was taken back to Paris and held in a vast, castle-like prison called the Temple. In its stone towers, King Louis XVI and his queen, Marie Antoinette, had once been held captive before they were sent to the guillotine during the French Revolution.

And it was there that Madame Guérin came to rescue him.

When he saw her, Victor turned pale and almost fainted. Madame Guérin hugged and caressed him, and "he suddenly revived and showed his delight by sharp cries, convulsive clenching of his hands, and a radiant expression," Dr. Itard wrote.

Dr. Itard wasn't there himself, but he heard about it later from people who were. "In the eyes of all," Itard wrote, "he appeared less like a fugitive obliged to return to the supervision of his keeper, than like an affectionate son who, of his own free will, comes and throws himself in the arms of the one who has given him life."

And so Victor came home.

Early the next morning, Dr. Itard came to see him. Victor sat up in bed. He held his arms toward his teacher, but Dr. Itard only gave him a cold stare. Victor covered his head with the bedclothes and began to cry. Dr. Itard reproached him "in a loud and threatening tone," until Victor was sobbing deeply. Then finally, Dr. Itard went and sat down on Victor's bed.

"This was always the signal of forgiveness," Itard wrote. "Victor understood me, made the first advances towards reconciliation, and all was forgotten."

*Those generous feelings . . . are the glory and happiness
of the human heart.*

—Jean-Marc-Gaspard Itard, *The Wild Boy of Aveyron*

STILL, DR. ITARD was not his teacher anymore. Victor
was no longer a boy. What could he do now? Where could
he go?

The other boys who had entered the Institute for Deaf-
Mutes at the same time as he were now out in the world,
plying the trades they'd learned at the Institute. Victor
could work—he liked doing tasks for people, especially

Madame Guérin—but he would never pass for an ordinary workman.

When he sawed logs for the fireplace, he always acted so overjoyed at the moment when the log was about to fall in two that someone who didn't know him would think he was a "raving maniac," Itard once wrote.

Around young women, he was unhappy and uneasy. Once, Itard saw him "sitting beside one of them and gently taking hold of her hand, her arms and knees until, feeling his restless desires increased instead of calmed by these odd caresses, and seeing no relief from his painful emotions in sight, he suddenly changed his attitude," and pushed the young woman away.

Another time, after caressing another young lady in the same, odd way, "he took the lady by her hands and drew her, without violence however, into the depths of an alcove.

There . . . showing in his manners and in his extraordinary facial expression an indescribable mixture of gaiety and sadness, of boldness and uncertainty, he several times solicited the lady's caresses by offering her his cheeks."

He held his face still, waiting for the kiss that did not come. He gave the young lady a hug and held her for a minute. Then he walked away.

Who these mysterious young women were was never written down. Julie came often to visit her mother at the Institute, so perhaps they were Julie's friends. Or maybe one of them was his old childhood friend, the astronomer's daughter.

Whoever they were, it does not seem that they were frightened of the peculiar young man. But still, there was no denying it: Victor was different from other people.

When a stormy wind blew, he still laughed out loud. He was still filled with joy and longing—and sometimes sadness—at the sight of a bright moon, a snow-covered field, a deep woods filled with light and shadow. . . .

Sometimes his unhappiness would turn to fury and he would cry out loud, tear his clothes, and even scratch or bite his beloved Madame Guérin, though he was always sorry afterward.

In short, he would never, ever be like other people.

Once, years before, when Victor was first beginning his studies, a Minister of the Interior named Jean-Antoine Chaptal (who took office after Lucien Bonaparte) had declared that the Savage, if he could not be educated, should be sent to a hospital for the insane called Charenton. If that had happened, Victor would have woken each morning for the rest of his life in a place where patients were given icy baths and confined by night in narrow boxes that held them tight as coffins. His fellow patients would have included a mad nobleman famous for his perversion and cruelty, the Marquis de Sade.

It hadn't happened then.

But what about now?

◆ ◆ ◆

Dr. Itard could have listened to the people who wanted to throw Victor into an insane asylum. He could have listened when people said Victor was nothing more than an idiot and that he — and his teacher — were utter failures.

But he didn't.

Instead, in a report he wrote to the current Minister of the Interior, Jean-Baptiste de Champagny, Dr. Itard pleaded for Victor's future.

He wrote that while it was true Victor had never learned to speak, he had become human in the way that really mattered. Victor, his teacher wrote, had overcome the obstacles his "destiny so strange" had set before him; he had become someone with "those generous feelings which are the glory and happiness of the human heart." He was, Itard wrote, an "extraordinary young man" who deserved the protection and care of others.

And for years afterward, Dr. Itard continued to defend his former pupil.

Because of Dr. Itard's pleading and steadfast support,

Victor was allowed to stay on at the Institute for Deaf-Mutes. He continued to live with Madame Guérin, as he had for so long.

And Julie still came to visit them.

Finally, in 1810, when Victor was twenty-two years old, Abbé Sicard and the administrators who oversaw the Institute for Deaf-Mutes decided it was time for him to find a new home.

They said that he couldn't be made to obey the Institute's rules. He did not belong in a place where "order and discipline" were important above all else.

And besides, the Institute for Deaf-Mutes now was only for boys. The administrators pointed out that Madame Guérin had a family who came to visit often, and girls were not welcome at the all-male Institute.

Neither were the curiosity seekers who still turned up from time to time, wanting to view the Savage.

So in the summer of 1811, when Victor was twenty-three,

he and Madame Guérin moved into their own little house. It was close by the Institute for Deaf-Mutes, so Dr. Itard could come visit. The government offered Madame Guérin a small pension for as long as Victor lived. She wrote a letter saying she accepted "with my deep gratitude" and signed it "Widow Guérin."

In another letter, she listed the things Victor would take with him: an old oaken bed, one mattress and a second straw mattress, a pillow, and a wool blanket.

Their house sat on a quiet, leafy street called the Feuillantines, close by an ancient convent that had been abandoned during the French Revolution. Inside the walls of the convent's vast, overgrown garden, birds sang and butterflies floated on the still air.

"A park, a wood, a stretch of open country . . . an avenue of chestnuts with room for a swing, and a dry quarry in which to play at soldiers . . . all the flowers one could possibly want, and what, to a child's eyes, was a virgin forest" is how the famous writer Victor Hugo described the convent grounds. The author, who was then only a boy, lived just a few doors down from Victor and Madame Guérin, and often played in the garden. Some say the hero of Hugo's book *The Hunchback of Notre Dame* may have been based on the young boy's glimpses of the strange, wild man who roamed the convent gardens and never spoke.

When he wandered the streets of Paris, people recognized him by his loping gait. They called him "le Sauvage," the Wild One.

In his quiet, peaceful life at house number four, Feuillantines, he could gather chestnuts from the woods. He could lie by the fire on a winter afternoon, or set out for the quarry and watch clouds race across the sky.

On a summer morning, he might be outside sawing firewood when the sky turned dark and the stormy wind blew, and what was to stop him from laughing out loud? As the rain

poured down and the wet earth released its scents, he might lope through the woods, stand by the quarry and pause for a minute, listening.

When autumn came, he could lean from a stone bridge over the Seine and watch the yellow leaves drift down the river or visit the horse market with its sweet-smelling hay. He could amble through sunny vineyards and up the slopes of Montmartre's high hill, where the windmills turned.

He could do whatever he wanted, for the rest of his life.

AFTERWORD

One day at their house at number four, Feuillantines, Madame Guérin and Victor had a visitor.

It was J.-J. Virey, the scientist who had written a report about Victor years earlier when he first came to the Institute for Deaf-Mutes.

Seventeen years had passed. Victor was twenty-nine now. The scientist was curious: Had the Savage *ever* learned to talk?

And the answer, of course, was no.

Maybe, as J.-J. Virey sat in their little house, Victor looked at him with fear. For how was Victor (or even Madame Guérin) to know the scientist hadn't come to take Victor away to be studied? After all, it had happened before.

Twice.

Maybe Victor and Madame Guérin were both relieved when, after a short visit, the scientist left.

In any case, all that J.-J. Virey thought worth noting down about Victor now was this: "Today he understands several things, without saying words. . . . He remains fearful, half wild, incapable of learning to speak, despite all the efforts that were made."

Dr. Itard once wrote that people looked at the wild boy without really seeing him, passed judgment on him without knowing him, and that after that, they "spoke no more about him."

And for the rest of Victor's life, that was true.

Victor died in the winter of 1828, when he would have been about forty years old, but we know that only because of a few lines published nearly twenty years later, when Dr. Itard died.

The article didn't say what caused Victor's death. It said only that at the time he died, he'd been living with Madame Guérin at number four, Feuillantines and that he'd been saved from being thrown into Bicêtre by his "protector," Dr. Itard.

The mist that hid his life had descended, deeper than ever, and this time it never lifted. Still, we know that Victor lived his whole life in freedom, close to the people he loved. We know he never ran away again—or at least, he always came back.

It never *did* take much to make him happy.

AUTHOR'S NOTE

This book is Victor's story told as it happened in his own time. For that reason, it doesn't touch on something that often comes up today: the question of whether the Wild Boy of Aveyron had a condition now known as autism.

It's true that some of the wild boy's traits—his rocking from side to side and his love of order, for example—are sometimes seen in children with autism. On the other hand, his well-documented ability to read other people's expressions is not typical of autistic children. Neither is the quick and intense attachment he showed for the people who cared for him during the course of his adventures.

I don't think we can ever know whether the wild boy was autistic, but in any event, I believe he deserves to be remembered as more than a case study.

And in the end, though he never learned to talk, the days and months and years he spent working so hard on his lessons were not wasted.

In later years, Dr. Itard took what he had learned with the wild boy and used it to develop new ways of teaching deaf children. Still later, a student of Itard's, a man named Édouard Séguin, used many of the same ideas to teach, for the first time ever, children once dismissed as "imbeciles" or "idiots."

"It is in the Memoirs on the education of the Wild Boy of Aveyron that Dr. Itard set down the true and the only seeds of positive education," Séguin wrote. Because of the wild boy, thousands and thousands of children who once would have been confined in boredom and misery in places like Bicêtre were sent to schools of their own and given a chance at a better life.

Later still, the famous educator Maria Montessori read Dr. Itard's work. She used it to help develop new teaching methods that influenced teachers around the world. Because of that, today's children enjoy more freedom to learn in their own way than they would have if one wild boy and his teacher had never met, so long ago in Paris.

SOURCE NOTES

pp. 1–4: Descriptions of the wild boy in the forest are based on the first eyewitness accounts of his sightings and captures and on later scientific observations. Many of these reports, such as Constans-Saint-Estève's letters and the scientific reports of Pierre-Joseph Bonnaterre and J.-J. Virey, are reprinted in Harlan Lane's *The Wild Boy of Aveyron.*

p. 1: walked upright: per the vast majority of reports. Scattered observations of the boy going on all fours seem have been made at times when he was very tired, scrambling up slopes, or taking off running. The scientist J.-J. Virey wrote, "I have examined his knees; they are no harder, more calloused, or more worn than any ordinary child's. It is very likely that he has always walked erect, except in a few rare instances and during infancy." (Virey in Lane, *Wild Boy*, p. 35).

p. 2: about nine years old: based on an orphanage administrator's estimate in 1800 that the boy "appears to be twelve years of age at most" (orphange official to *Journal des débats*, January 1800, Ibid., p. 10)

p. 5: "Everyone came . . . wild beast": Constans-Saint-Estève, *Journal des débats*, January 1800, Ibid., p. 7.

pp. 5–7: The dates and basic outline of the wild boy's early sightings and captures follow Lane, pp. 6–7.

pp. 13–14: For Guiraud's report, see Shattuck, pp. 19–20.

p. 14: red tile roof and wooden balconies: Vidal's workshop outside Saint-Sernin is still standing, surrounded by terraced gardens.

p. 15: "I will shortly . . . extraordinary being": Constans-Saint-Estève, *Journal des débats*, January 1800, in Lane, *Wild Boy*, p. 10.

p. 15: "I found him . . . great pleasure" Ibid., p. 7.

p. 16: The strange boy's eyes . . . couldn't quite read: Foulquier-Lavergne, p. 12.

pp. 16 and 18: "resisted vigorously" and "great impatience": Constans-Saint-Estève, *Journal des débats*, January 1800, in Lane, *Wild Boy*, p. 8.

p. 19: "I had a hard time catching him" and "air of satisfaction that nothing could trouble": Ibid., p. 8.

pp. 20–21: "I have ordered brought . . . unidentified child," "In every respect . . .

philanthropic observer," "I am informing the government," and "Would you see to it . . . which he cannot escape": Ibid., p. 9.

p. 22: "A young savage, found in the woods near Saint Sernin. Deaf and mute.": Saint-Affrique orphanage roll book, Archives Départementales de l'Aveyron.

p. 22: "He took to running . . . and disappeared": orphanage official to *Journal des débats*, January 1800, in Lane, *Wild Boy*, p. 10.

p. 24: "feeble in spirit": Saint-Affrique orphanage roll book, Archives Départementales de l'Aveyron.

p. 25: "His eyes are dark . . . means of escape" and "We made him a gown . . . lets out sharp cries": orphanage official to *Journal des débats*, January 1800, in Lane, *Wild Boy*, p. 10.

p. 26: "From external appearance . . . pleasant smile": Bonnaterre, Ibid., p. 33.

p. 29: "It was only with some difficulty . . . Central School": Aveyron commissioner J.-P. Randon to Constans-Saint-Estève, February 5, 1800, Ibid., p. 15.

p. 30: "When he raises his head . . . cutting instrument," "There is one . . . left cheek," "His whole body is covered with scars," and "Did some barbaric hand . . . death-dealing blade?": Bonnaterre, Ibid., p. 34.

p. 32: For Bonnaterre's account of these wild children, see Gineste, pp. 182–193.

pp. 33–34: "The sounds of the most harmonious . . . turn around to seize them": Bonnaterre in Lane, *Wild Boy*, p. 39.

p. 34: "He has been seen, when tired, to walk on all fours": Ibid., p. 47.

p. 36: "He is always looking . . . distance from the town": Ibid., p. 44.

p. 37: "When it is time . . . furious if not obeyed": Ibid., p. 46.

p. 37: "His sleep . . . pain or pleasure": Ibid., p. 45.

p. 37: as though he were having a seizure: Ibid., p. 36.

p. 38: "This eagerness . . . just experienced,": Ibid., p. 44.

pp. 39–40: "I could not imagine . . . impressions of heat," "One evening . . . rid of these garments," "Next I pretended . . . the school building," and "Instead of showing . . . repeated yanks": Ibid., p. 44.

p. 41: "comfortably warm": Ibid., p. 45.

p. 41: "He can be indifferent . . . with the same habits": Ibid., p. 44.

p. 42: Clair's age and origin: baptismal records for the village of Connac, May 9, 1736, Archives Départementales de l'Aveyron.

pp. 45–46: "He was constantly occupied . . . the most practiced man," "He opened the pods . . . movement," "As he emptied . . . nearby coals," and "When he felt . . . cooking oil was stored": Bonnaterre in Lane, *Wild Boy*, pp. 39–40.

p. 46: "I saw him . . . without being caught": Ibid., p. 41.

pp. 46–47: "a captain of the auxiliary . . . sausage on the plate": Ibid., p. 40.

p. 47: "His affections . . . satisfying his needs": Ibid., p. 39.

p. 48: "Suspicion of imbecility": Ibid., p. 41.

p. 48: "This child . . . reflects on nothing," "no imagination, no memory," and "This state of imbecility . . . and determination": Ibid., pp. 41–42.

p. 49: "Unfortunate boy" and "I claim him . . . forthwith": February 1, 1800, Bonaparte to Aveyron commissioner J.-P. Randon, Ibid., p. 14.

p. 51: "Provided that the state of imbecility . . . kind of education": Bonnaterre, Ibid., p. 47.

p. 52: "Whenever we changed . . . dearest affection": Ibid., p. 41.

pp. 53-54: old maps of the time: Arbellot, p. 46.

p. 53: "putting his chin . . . up to his mouth": Bonnaterre in Lane, *Wild Boy*, p. 47.

pp. 53–54: "During our trip . . . attempts at escape": Ibid., p. 44.

p. 54: Description of Clermont: Young, Arthur. *Arthur Young's Travels in France During the Years 1787, 1788, 1789.* Matilda Betham-Edwards, ed. London: George Bell and Sons, 1909. Library of Economics and Liberty. http://www.econlib.org/library/YPDBooks/Young/yngTF.html. Entry for August 11, 1789 (¶4.75) "Clermont is in the midst of a most curious country, all volcanic; and is built and paved with lava: much of it forms one of the worst built, dirtiest, and most stinking places I have met with. There are many streets that can, for blackness, dirt, and ill scents, only be represented by narrow channels cut in a night dunghill. The contention of nauseous savours, with which the air is impregnated, when brisk mountain gales do not ventilate these excrementitious lanes, made me envy the nerves of the good people, who, for what I know, may be happy in them."

p. 54: pestered by "curious people . . . along our route" [*l'importunité dae curieux qui se portaient en foule sur notre route*]: Bonnaterre to Aveyron official, September 2, 1800, in Gineste, p. 145.

p. 56: "He refused to eat . . . any medicine" and "He recovered very well in a few days": J.-J. Virey in Lane, *Wild Boy*, p. 46.

p. 58: "arrived . . . Bonnaterre": *Gazette de France*, August 9, 1800, in Shattuck, p. 190.

p. 58: "As yet we know . . . visited promptly" and "down to . . . first thoughts": *Gazette de France*, August 9, 1800, in Lane, *Wild Boy*, p. 18.

p. 58: "in the hands . . . deaf-mutes": *Gazette de France*, August 9, 1800, in Shattuck, p. 190.

p. 60: "Many people . . . past life": Itard, p. 4.

p. 62: "a certain amount of ill-natured treatment" from "children his own age": Ibid., p. 11.

p. 62: "He detests children . . . without fail": Virey in Lane, *Wild Boy*, p. 42.

p. 64: "He likes solitude . . . as much as possible" and "If he is afraid . . . and remain alone": Virey, Ibid., p. 43.

p. 64: "The Savage of Aveyron, currently at the Institute for Deaf-Mutes" [*Le Sauvage de l'Averyon, actuellement à l'Institution des Sourds-Muets*]: Archives Départementales de l'Aveyron.

p. 65: "annoyed and victimized . . . just as much": Itard in Shattuck, p. 29.

p. 68: "he stood at the window . . . countryside" and "Sometimes he dreams . . . during the day": Virey in Lane, *Wild Boy*, p. 45.

p. 68: "young savage of Aveyron" [*le jeune sauvage de l'Averyon*]: Bonaparte to Abbé Sicard, August 29, 1800, in Gineste, p. 144.

p. 69: One person who saw the wild boy . . . door and windows [*Il a . . . un balancement . . . qui ressemble à celui de l'ours de la ménagerie . . . ses yeux se portaient d'une manière inquiète vers la porte où les fenêtres.*]: le *Courrier des spectacles*, September 2, 1800, in Gineste, p. 478.

p. 69: "lively joy" [*vif sentiment de joie*]: le *Publiciste*, September 2, 1800, in Gineste, p. 477.

p. 69: "very lively cries of joy" [*des cris de joie très vifs*]: le *Courrier des spectacles*, September 2, 1800, in Gineste, p. 478.

p. 70: married and widowed twice: death certificate of Clair Saussol, Rodez, February 28, 1822, Archives Départementales de l'Aveyron.

p. 70: "his old guardian, whom he appears to love very much": *Gazette de France*, August 9, 1800, in Lane, *Wild Boy*, p. 18.

p. 71: Often, he went hungry: Itard, p. 88. When he could get food . . . by himself: Ibid., p. 19. Locked in a dark closet: Ibid., p. 95.

p. 71: about forty boys and twenty girls: Institute for Deaf-Mutes enrollment records, 1801, National Archives, Paris.

pp. 71–72: For descriptions of student life at the Institute, see Harlan Lane's *When the Mind Hears: A History of the Deaf*, pp. 8–13. The separate gardens for girls and boys can be seen in contemporary floor plans in unedited manuscripts in the archives of the Institute for Deaf-Mutes, now known as the Institut National de Jeunes Sourds de Paris.

p. 73: "The child . . . interesting being": Itard, p. xxiv.

p. 74: "I have often . . . this situation": Ibid., p. 13.

p. 74: "condemned . . . in our asylums": Philippe Pinel, "Report to the Société des Observateurs de l'Homme concerning the child known by the name of 'Sauvage de l'Aveyron,'" in Lane, *Wild Boy*, p. 58.

p. 76: "Debtors are incarcerated . . . epileptics, imbeciles. . . ." Mercier, p. 160.

p. 76: "subterranean dungeons . . . in the roof": Ibid., p. 163.

p. 76: "to tear a child . . . boredom in an institution": Itard, p. 11.

p. 77: "I never shared this unfavorable opinion" and "I dared to conceive certain hopes": Ibid., p. 7.

p. 78: "I believed . . . tastes and inclinations": Ibid., p. 11.

pp. 79–80: "all the patience . . . enlightened teacher," "It was necessary . . . happy in his own way," "sleeping, eating . . . the fields," and "scampers": Ibid., p. 12.

p. 82: "I have many . . . great satisfaction": Ibid., p. 64.

pp. 82–83: "was the beginning . . . signs of satisfaction" and "I shall perhaps . . . life's earliest joys": Ibid., pp. 24 and 25.

p. 83: "A ray of sun . . . child of nature": Ibid., p. 18.

p. 83: "cry of joy": Ibid., p. 12.

p. 84: "There, giving vent . . . incredible eagerness": Ibid., p. 13.

p. 87: ". . . in moments of great happiness": Ibid., p. 33.

p. 89: "an almost ordinary child who cannot speak": Ibid., p. 49.

p. 89: "People may say . . . childish play": Ibid., p. 25.

p. 90–91: "He is often heard . . . sweetness" and "I am somewhat . . . name of Julie": Ibid., p. 33.

pp. 91–93: Victor's friendship with the astronomer's daughter: editors' note to article in *Décade philosophique,* 1800, in Gineste, p. 481.

p. 93: "in moments of great happiness": Itard, p. 33.

p. 94: "Everything put . . . communication of ideas": Ibid., p. 67.

pp. 94–95: "I have . . . shown him toys . . . before his bonfire": Ibid., p. 20.

p. 97: "It would have been inhuman to insist further": Ibid., p. 31.

p. 98: "despairing of success": Ibid., p. 32.

pp. 101–102: "trembling in every limb . . . towards the door," "With every appearance of anger," "his head directly . . . the chasm," and "He was pale . . . bed and wept": Ibid., p. 44.

p. 102: "contented himself . . . in tears": Ibid., p. 45.

p. 104: But after that day, Victor . . . ran away: Ibid., pp. 44–45.

p. 104: "escaped," "shed many tears on seeing her again," and "When Madame Guérin . . . began to weep": Ibid., pp. 24–25.

p. 105: "The child . . . early success": Ibid., p. 48.

p. 111: "There is always the same . . . stormy wind": Ibid., p. 92.

pp. 112–113: "such was the effect . . . wild than ever," "an independent life, happy and regretted," and "straight and regular . . . wild nature is composed": Ibid., pp. 23–24.

p. 114: "garland of flowers . . . swans": Edmond and Jules de Goncourt, in Herriot, p. 25.

pp. 114–116: "Madame Récamier . . . child of nature," "the young savage . . . attracted," "startling greed," "all the delicacies he could filch," "running across . . . rabbit," and "bundled into . . . nature untamed": L. C. Wairy, *Mémoires sur la vie privée de Napoléon, sa famille, et sa cour,* vol. 3, Paris: Ladvocat, 1830, in Lane, *Wild Boy,* pp. 108–109.

p. 119: "I was obliged . . . does he not speak?": Itard, p. 26.

p. 119: "inspiration of really creative imagination": Ibid., p. 78.

p. 119: "the most rapid . . . first triumph": Ibid., p. 32.

p. 121: "this reading conveyed no meaning to him": Ibid., p. 61.

p. 121: "He often stopped . . . of his errand": Ibid., pp. 71–72.

p. 122: "I have seen . . . threat, or punishment": Ibid., p. 91.

p. 122: "stamp with joy . . . behind his head": Ibid., p. 57.

pp. 122–124: "Thus we have instructor . . . grimacing their hardest": Ibid., p. 86.

p. 124: "'Unhappy creature . . . boredom at Bicêtre": Ibid., p. 73.

p. 124: "scarcely had I finished . . . bitter grief": Ibid., p. 74.

p. 126: "To speak of . . . judgment on him": Ibid., p. 52.

p. 127: "I know, sir . . . diligent" and "essential . . . know the results": Champagny to Itard, June 13, 1806, in Lane, *Wild Boy,* p. 133 (date in Gineste, p. 390).

p. 127: "brilliant hopes": Itard, p. 40.

p. 127: "As for me . . . and to distain": Ibid., p. 52.

p. 128: "incurable dumbness": Ibid., p. 86.

p. 129: "As soon as his governess . . . to go out": Ibid., p. 93.

p. 131: "Hurrying into the street . . . Barrière d'Enfer": Ibid., p. 93.

p. 134: "From my window . . . wealth of foliage" and "Along all . . . century-old trees": Victorien Sardou, in preface to Cain, p. xx.

p. 136: half a million people: Braudel, p. 248.

p. 137: "He turned in the direction . . . gained the forest": Itard, p. 89.

pp. 141–142: "he suddenly revived . . . radiant expression," "In the eyes . . . given him life," "in a loud and threatening tone," and "This was always . . . all was forgotten": Ibid., p. 90.
p. 143: "Those generous . . . human heart": Ibid., p. 87.

p. 144: "raving maniac": Ibid., p. 92.

p. 144: "sitting beside . . . changed his attitude" and "he took the lady . . . his cheeks": Ibid., p. 97.

p. 146: the Savage . . . should be sent to . . . Charenton: Chaptal to the Administrators of Charitable Institutions (including the administrators of the Institute for Deaf-Mutes), April 8, 1801, in Gineste, pp. 265–266.

p. 147: "destiny so strange": Itard, p. 101.

p. 147: "those generous feelings which are the glory and happiness of the human heart": Ibid., p. 87.

p. 147: "extraordinary young man": Ibid., p. 101.

p. 148: "order and discipline" *[l'ordre et la discipline]*: Administrators of Charitable Institutions to the Minister of the Interior, July 13, 1810, in Gineste, p. 448.

p. 149: "with my deep gratitude" *[de ma profonde reconnaissance]* and "Widow Guérin" *[Veuve Guérin]*: Madame Guérin to the administrators of the Institute for Deaf-Mutes, May 2, 1811, Ibid., p. 454.

p. 149: list of Victor's possessions: Madame Guérin to the administrators of the Institute for Deaf-Mutes, July 10, 1811, Ibid.

p. 149–150: "A park, a wood . . . virgin forest": Hugo in Maurois, p. 20.

p. 150: recognized him by his loping gait: Shattuck, p. 156.

p. 154: "Today he understands . . . efforts that were made" *[Aujourd'hui il comprend plusieurs choses, sans articuler des mots. . . . Il est resté effaré, à demi sauvage et n'a pu apprendre à parler, malgré les soins qu'on en a pris.]*: Virey, report of 1817, in Gineste, p. 455.

p. 154: "spoke no more about him": Itard, pp. 4–5.

p. 154: "protector" *[protecteur]*: E. Morel, "Notice biographique sur le Dr. Itard," *Annales de l'éducation des sourds-muets et des aveugles*, 1845, in Gineste, p. 455.

p. 157: "It is in the Memoirs . . . positive education": Séguin in Lane, *Wild Boy*, p. 269.

BIBLIOGRAPHY

Arbellot, Guy, et al. *Atlas de la Révolution française.* Vol. 1, *Routes et communications.* Paris: École des Hautes Études en Sciences Sociales, 1987.

Bonnaterre, P.-J. *Notice historique sur le sauvage de l'Aveyron.* Paris: Panckoucke, 1800. Translated by Harlan Lane and reprinted in his *The Wild Boy of Aveyron,* pp. 33–48.

Braudel, Fernand. *The Identity of France.* Vol. I, *History and Environment.* Translated by Siân Reynolds. New York: Harper and Row, 1988.

Cain, Georges. *Nooks and Corners of Old Paris.* London: E. G. Richards, 1907.

Foulquier-Lavergne, P. *Le Sauvage de l'Aveyron.* Rodez: Imprimerie de Broca, 1875.

Gineste, Thierry. *Victor de l'Aveyron: Dernier enfant sauvage, premier enfant fou.* Paris: Hachette/Pluriel, 1993.

Herriot, Édouard. *Madame Récamier.* Translated by Alys Hallard. New York: Boni and Liveright/London: Heinmann, 1926.

Itard, Jean-Marc-Gaspard. *The Wild Boy of Aveyron.* Translated by George and Muriel Humphrey. New York: Meredith, 1962.

———. *When the Mind Hears: A History of the Deaf.* New York: Random House, 1984.

Lane, Harlan. *The Wild Boy of Aveyron.* Cambridge, Massachusetts: Harvard University Press, 1976.

Maurois, André. *Olympio: The Life of Victor Hugo.* Translated by Gerard Hopkins. New York: Harper, 1956.

Mercier, Louis-Sébastien. *Panorama of Paris: Selections from Le Tableau de Paris.* Based on the translation by Helen Simpson. Jeremy D. Popkin, ed. University Park, PA: The Pennsylvania State University Press, 1999.

Shattuck, Roger. *The Forbidden Experiment: The Story of the Wild Boy of Aveyron.* London: Quartet Books, 1980.

Index

affection, 47, 70, 82
anger, 36–37
autism, 157

Bicêtre, 76
Bonaparte, Lucien, 49–50, 68–69, 126–27
Bonnaterre, Pierre-Joseph, 26–28
   journey to Paris, 51–55
   studies of wild boy, 29–50

Champagny, Jean-Baptiste de, 127, 147
Chaptal, Jean-Antoine, 146
Charenton, 146
Clermont, 54
clothes, 10, 80
cold temperatures, 38–41, 79–80
Constans-Saint-Estève, J.-J., 15–21
crying, 102

deaf-mutes, 50, 58–59
deafness, 22

escape
   attempt during trip to Paris, 53–54
   attempts from Central School, 35–36
   from Institute for Deaf-Mutes, 129–41
   from Lacaune, 8, 11
   from Madame Guérin, 104

fire, 38–39

food, 8, 12, 17–18, 45–47, 51–53

Guérin, Julie, 90–91, 117, 145, 148
Guérin, Madame, 79, 82–83, 87, 93, 104, 105–10, 112, 128–29
   moves into a cottage with Victor, 148–49
   rescues Victor from prison, 139–41
Guérin, Monsieur, 79, 87, 90, 128

happiness, 19, 79, 83–84, 93
Homo ferus, 32

imbecile, 48, 74
insane asylum, 74, 76, 146–47
Institute for Deaf-Mutes, 50, 60–72, 119, 120, 127, 148
intelligence, 16, 48
Itard, Jean-Marc-Gaspard, 73–74, 76–86, 88–89
   death of, 154
   pleas for Victor's future, 147–48
   teaches Victor to communicate, 98–102
   teaches Victor to say words, 96–98
   tries to teach Victor to talk, 120–25
   welcomes Victor home, 141–42

Lacaune, 4, 5, 6, 9–10

Mercier, Louis-Sébastien, 76
mirror, 32–33
Montessori, Maria, 157
Moulins, 55
music, 33

ACKNOWLEDGMENTS

I would like to thank the many, many people who read (or listened to) drafts and offered advice and encouragement, with special thanks to Dan Bachhuber's fourth-, fifth-, and sixth-grade classes at the J. J. Hill Montessori School in St. Paul, Minnesota; the Jerome Foundation, whose Travel and Study Grant Program enabled me to retrace the wild boy's footsteps in France; Charles Eisendrath of the Knight-Wallace Journalism Fellowship at the University of Michigan, who helped me find a new writing path; Monsieur Jean Delmas, longtime director of the Rodez archives, who told me so much about the wild boy; Harlan Lane, whose book *The Wild Boy of Aveyron* was invaluable to me in writing this one; my agent, George Nicholson, who believed in this book; and most of all my wonderful husband, Don, who liked the wild boy as much as I did.

English Channel

Atlantic
Ocean

THE
WILD BOY'S
JOURNEY

0   miles   100

Bay of Biscay